The Mind of Christ

The Mind of Christ

John R. MacDuff

Edited and Mildly Modernized by
Ralph I. Tilley

Life in the Spirit Books
P.O. Box 405
Sellersburg, Indiana 47172

The Mind of Christ
John R. MacDuff
Edited and mildly modernized by Ralph I. Tilley
Copyright © 2013
Ralph I. Tilley

Scripture quotations marked (ESV) are from *The Holy Bible, English Standard Version®* (ESV®), copyright © 2001 by Crossway, a publishing ministry of Good News Publishers. Used by permission. All rights reserved.

Cover photo: attributed to Rembrandt (Rembrandt Harmenszoon van Rijn) (1606 – 1669), circa 1655; in the public domain.

This edited volume of *The Mind of Christ* is published by Life in the Spirit Books, a ministry of Life in the Spirit Ministries, Inc.

Life in the Spirit
P.O. Box 405
Sellersburg, Indiana 47172

www.litsjournal.org
editor@litsjournal.org

ISBN-13: 978-0-578-11878-9
ISBN-10: 0-578-11878-5

To the Lord Jesus Christ,

whose likeness is ardently pursued

by every thirsty-hearted follower.

Contents

Introduction

The purpose of God from eternity past is that every authentic Christian would eventually bear the likeness of God's very own Son, the Lord Jesus Christ: "For those whom he foreknew he also predestined to be conformed to the image of his Son . . ." (Rom. 8:29, ESV).

The death, resurrection, ascension, and present mediatorial work of Christ are God's salvation initiatives and gracious redemptive actions, and the foundational work for the Holy Spirit's sanctifying ministry on earth. The Holy Spirit is Christ's gift to the Church and effective agent in the lives of Christ's disciples, providing the inner dynamic power for each believer to become increasingly conformed to the Lord Jesus: "And we all, with unveiled face, beholding the glory of the Lord, are being transformed into the same image from one degree of glory to another. For this comes from the Lord who is the Spirit" (2 Cor. 3:18, ESV).

To be renewed by the Spirit day-by-day is God's desire for his people and the privilege of each Christian. The apostle Paul testified to a personal, daily, spiritual renewal occurring in the innermost sanctuary of his being: "Though our outer self is wasting away, our inner self is being renewed day by day" (2 Cor. 4:16, ESV).

Spiritual renewal is the work of the Holy Spirit. However, while daily renewal is the work of the Spirit, God uses a variety of *means* to assist us in his renewing activities. In addition to the sacred Scriptures, God has used for over two thousand years the spiritual writings of some of his gifted saints to help us along the way. One person whose writings God has used to bless Christ's Church for the past century is John Ross MacDuff, the author of this devotional book.

John R. MacDuff

John Ross MacDuff (1818-1895) was born May 23, 1818, at Bonhard, near Perth, Scotland. After studying at the University of Edinburgh, he became in 1842 parish minister of Kettins, Forfarshire; in 1849 of St. Madoes, Perthshire; and in 1855 of Sandyford, Glasgow. He received the Doctor of Divinity degree from the University of Glasgow in 1862, and about the same time also from the University of New York. He retired from pastoral work in 1871 and thereafter lived at Chislehurst, Kent, for the purpose of focusing entirely on writing.

MacDuff was a prolific author of devotional works, as well as a composer of hymns. He served as a pastor for many years, including as a minister in the Church of Scotland. Several of his writings are still in circulation; some of the best known are: *The Prophet of Fire, Memories of Bethany, Memories of Gennesaret, The Shepherd and His Flock, Sunset on the Hebrew Mountains, Comfort Ye, The Golden Gospel, Morning and Night Watches,* and *The Mind of Christ.*

The Book

There are several editions of this book on the Internet in the form of e-books, which prove to be a blessing to multiplied thousands of readers. However, since I first came across this devotional by MacDuff, I became increasingly convinced that it deserved to be reprinted, although I felt the language needed to be edited and mildly modernized. This I have done.

In addition to updating the language of the book, I have also included Bible references, which were absent in MacDuff's original text. However, I have retained his use of the King James Version of the Bible—to have done otherwise would have obscured many of his comments. The reader must be advised that in MacDuff's quotation of Scripture, he quite often is imprecise, sometimes rephrasing the word order, sometimes changing verb tenses. Additionally,

I have inserted at the conclusion of each devotional a verse or two from a classic hymn.

While there are many devotionals available for today's Christian, and many good ones at that, sometimes it is helpful to read a new one—from a different perspective. As my soul has been fed by the Spirit through MacDuff's devotional, I have been repeatedly impressed with his saintliness, his breadth of biblical knowledge, his spiritual discernment and insight—and his flaming passion for the Lord Jesus Christ. Here was a man of God who was spiritually alive and lived his life to the glory and praise of the living God. Much of his life was spent in stimulating believers—through his voice and pen—to rise up and "possess their possessions," given through the Lord Jesus.

Acknowledgments
This book was published in America by Robert Carter and Brothers in 1860. It has been digitized in recent years by the Project Gutenberg. Additionally, I am once again indebted to my handy and willing proofreaders: my wife Emily and our daughter Rochelle Farah. They do a great job in catching my typos—as long as I don't insert further material *after* they have proofed my work!

Life in the Spirit Books
Our book, booklets, and brochures are distributed through our ministry on a *donation* basis. The suggested donation prices are kept at a very modest rate in order to make them readily affordable. This organization exists for the purpose of ministry—not money!

My Prayer
It is my prayer that the same Spirit who guided John R. MacDuff in writing *The Mind of Christ*—and who indwells every believer—will now renew your own mind as you prayerfully read the following thirty-one devotionals, until the mind of the Lord Jesus will increasingly become your own mind.

Ralph I. Tilley
Soli Deo Gloria

Author's Preface

The mind of Jesus! What a study is this! To attain a dim reflection of it, is the ambition of angels—higher they can not soar. "To be conformed to the image of His Son" (Rom. 8:29)—it is the end of God in the predestination of His Church from all eternity. "We shall be like Him!" (1 Jn. 3:2)—it is the Bible picture of heaven!

In a former little volume, we pondered some of the gracious words which proceeded out of the mouth of Jesus. In the present, we have a few faint outlines of that holy character which constituted the living exposition and embodiment of his precepts.

But how lofty such a standard! How all creature-perfection shrinks abashed and confounded before a divine portraiture like this! He is the true "angel standing in the sun" (Rev. 19:17), who alone projects no shadow; so bathed in the glories of deity that likeness to him becomes like the light in which he is shrouded—no man can approach unto it. May we not, however, seek at least to approximate, though we can not adequately resemble? It is impossible on earth to associate with a fellow-being without getting, in some degree, assimilated to him. So, the more we study "the mind of Christ," the more we are in his company—holding converse with Him as our best and dearest friend—observing his holy looks and holy deeds—the more shall we be "transformed into the same image" (2 Cor. 3:18).

"Consider," says the Great Apostle (literally "gaze on"), "Christ Jesus" (Heb. 3:1). Study feature by feature, outline by outline, of that Peerless Exemplar. "Gaze" on the Sun of Righteousness, till, like gazing long on the natural sun, you carry away with you, on your spiritual vision, dazzling images of his brightness and glory. Though He be the Archetype of all goodness, remember he is no shadowy model—though the Infinite Yahweh, he was "the man Christ Jesus" (1 Tim. 2:5).

We must never, indeed, forget that it is not the mind, but the work of Immanuel, which lies at the foundation of a sinner's hope. He must be known as a Savior, before he is studied as an Example. His doing and dying is the center jewel, of which all the virtues of his holy life are merely the setting. But neither must we overlook the Scripture obligation to walk in his footsteps and imbibe his Spirit, for "if any man have not the Spirit of Christ, he is none of him" (Rom. 8:9).

Oh, that each individual Christian were more Savior-like! That, in the manifestation of a holy character and heavenly demeanor, it might be said in some feeble measure of the weak and imperfect reflection—"Such was Jesus!"

How far short we are of such a criterion, mournful experience can testify. But it is at least comforting to know that there is a day coming, when, in the full vision and fruition of the Glorious Original, the exhortation of our motto-verse will be needed no more; when we shall be able to say, in the words of an inspired apostle, "We have the MIND OF CHRIST" (1 Cor. 2:16).

John R. MacDuff

- *Day 1* -
Compassion

"I have compassion on the multitude . . ."
Mark 8:2

What a pattern to his people—the tender compassion of Jesus!

Jesus found the world he came to save a moral Bethesda. The wail of suffering humanity was everywhere borne to his ear. It was his delight to walk its porches, to pity, relieve, comfort, save! The faintest cry of misery arrested his footsteps—stirred a ripple in this fountain of infinite love.

Was it a leper—that dreaded name which entailed a life-long exile from friendly looks and kindly words? There was One, at least, who had tones and deeds of tenderness for the outcast. "Jesus, being moved with compassion, put forth his hand, and touched him" (Mk. 1:41). Was it some blind beggars on the Jericho highway, groping in darkness, pleading for help? "Jesus stood still, and had compassion on them, and touched their eyes!" (Mt. 20:32, 34). Was it the speechless pleadings of a widow's tears at the gate of Nain, when she followed her earthly pride and joy to the grave? "When the Lord saw her, he had compassion on her, and said, 'Weep not!'" (Lk. 7:13).

Even when he rebukes, the bow of compassion is seen in the cloud, or rather, that cloud, as it passes, dissolves in a rain shower of mercy. He pronounces Jerusalem "desolate," but the doom is uttered amid a flood of anguished sorrow!

Reader, do the compassionate words and deeds of a tender Savior find any feeble echo and transcript in yours? As you traverse in thought the wastes of human wretchedness, does the spectacle give rise, not to the mere emotional feeling which weeps itself away in sentimental tears, but to an earnest desire to do something to mitigate the sufferings of woe-worn humanity?

How vast and worldwide the claims on your compassion—now near, now at a distance—the unmet and unanswered cry of perishing millions abroad, the heathen which lie helpless at your own door, the public charity languishing, the mission staff dwarfed and crippled from lack of necessary funds, a suffering community, a starving family, a poor neighbor, a helpless orphan, it may be, some crowded hovel, where misery and vice run riot, or some lonely sick chamber, where the dim lamp has been wasting for dreary nights, or some desolate home which death has entered, where "Joseph is not, and Simeon is not" (Gen 42:36), and where some sobbing heart, under the tattered garment of poverty, mourns, uncomforted and unpitied.

Are there none such within your reach, to whom a trifling pittance would be as an angel of mercy? How it would hallow and enhance all you possess, were you to seek to live as gracious distributor of God's bounties! If he has given you of this world's substance, remember it is bestowed, not to be greedily hoarded or lavishly squandered. Property and wealth are talents to be exchanged and given for the good of others—sacred trusts, not selfishly to be enjoyed, but generously to be employed.

The poor are the representatives of Jesus, their needs he considers as his own, and he will recompense accordingly. The feeblest expression of Christian pity and love, though it be but the widow's mite, or the cup of cold water, or the kindly look and word when there is neither mite nor cup to give, yet, if done in his name, it is entered into the Book of Life as a "loan to the Lord" (1 Sam. 2:20). And in that day when "the books are opened" (Rev. 20:12), the loan will be paid back with interest.

Arm yourselves likewise with the same mind!

Love divine, all loves excelling,
Joy of heaven to earth come down;
Fix in us thy humble dwelling;
All thy faithful mercies crown!

Jesus, Thou art all compassion,
Pure unbounded love Thou art;
Visit us with Thy salvation;
Enter every trembling heart.

— Charles Wesley (1707-1788)

- *Day 2* -
Submission in Trial

"Not my will, but Thine, be done."
Luke 22:42

Where was there ever submission like this!

The life of Jesus was one long martyrdom. From Bethlehem's manger to Calvary's cross, there was scarce one break in the clouds; these gathered more darkly and ominously around him till they burst over his devoted head as he uttered his expiring cry. Yet throughout this pilgrimage of sorrow, no murmuring accent escaped his lips. The most suffering of all suffering lives was one of uncomplaining submission. "Not my will, but Thy will," was the motto of this wondrous Being!

When he came into the world he thus announced his advent, "Lo, I come, I delight to do Thy will, O my God" (Heb. 10:7, 9). When he left it, we listen to the same prayer of blended agony and acquiescence, "O my Father, if it be possible let this cup pass from me! Nevertheless not as I will, but as Thou wilt" (Mt. 36:39).

Reader, is this mind also in you? Ah, what are your trials compared to his! What are the ripples in your tide of woe, compared to the waves and billows which swept over him! If he, the spotless Lamb of God, murmured not, how can you murmur? His were the sufferings of a bosom never once darkened with the passing shadow of guilt or sin. Your severest sufferings are deserved, yea, infinitely less than deserved! Are you tempted to indulge in hard suspicions as to God's faithfulness and love, in appointing some peculiar trial? Ask yourself, Would Jesus have done this? Should I seek to pry into the deep things of God, when he, in the spirit of a weaned child, was satisfied with the solution, "Even so, Father, for so it seems good in Thy sight" (Lk. 10:21)?

"Even so, Father!" Afflicted one, "tossed with tempest, and not comforted" (Isa. 54:11), take that word on which your Lord pillowed his suffering head, and make it, as he did, the secret of your submission.

The sick child will take the bitterest drink from a father's hand. "This cup which Thou, O God, givest me to drink, shall I not drink it" (Jn. 18:11)? Be it mine to lie passive in the arms of your chastening love, exulting in the assurance that all your appointments, though sovereign, are never arbitrary, but that there is a gracious "need be" in them all. My Father, my covenant God, the God who spared not Jesus! It may well hush every repining word.

Drinking deep of his sweet spirit of submission, you will be able thus to meet, yea, even to welcome, your sorest cross, saying, "Yes, Lord, all is well, just because it is your blessed will. Take me, use me, chasten me, as it seems good in your sight. My will is resolved into yours. This trial is dark; I can not see the why and the wherefore of it—but not my will, but your will! The gourd is withered (see Jon. 4:7); I can not see the reason of so speedy a dissolution of the loved earthly shelter; sense and sight ask in vain why these leaves of earthly refreshment have been doomed so soon to droop in sadness and sorrow. But it is enough. 'The Lord prepared the worm' (Jon. 4:7)—'not my will, but your will!'"

Oh, how does the stricken soul honor God by thus being silent in the midst of dark and perplexing dealings, recognizing in these part of the needed discipline and training for a sorrowless, sinless, deathless world. Such a soul regards every trial as a link in the chain which draws it to heaven, where the whitest robes will be found to be those here baptized with suffering and bathed in tears!

Arm yourselves likewise with the same mind!

My stubborn will at last hath yielded;
I would be Thine, and Thine alone;
And this the prayer my lips are bringing,
Lord, let in me Thy will be done.

— Leila N. Morris (1862-1929)

- *Day 3* -
Devotion to God

"Wist ye not that I must be about my Father's business?"
Luke 2:49

"My meat is to do the will of him that sent me, and to finish his work" (Jn. 4:34). That one object brought Jesus from heaven—that one object he pursued with unflinching, undeviating constancy, until he could say, "It is finished" (Jn. 19:30).

However short man comes of his "chief end," Glory to God in the highest was the motive, the rule, and exponent of every act of that wondrous life. With us, the magnet of the soul, even when truest, is ever subject to partial oscillations and depressions, trembling at times away from its great attraction point. His never knew one tremulous wavering from its all-glorious center. With him there were no ebbs and flows, no fits and starts. He could say, in the words of that prophetic psalm which speaks so preeminently of himself, "I have set the Lord always before me" (Psa. 16:8).

Reader, do you feel that in some feeble measure this lofty life-motto of the sinless Son of God is written on your home and heart, regulating your actions, chastening your joys, quickening your hopes, giving energy and direction to your whole being, subordinating all the affections of your nature to their high destiny? With pure and unalloyed motives, with a single eye, and a single aim, can you say, somewhat in the spirit of his brightest follower, "This one thing I do" (Phil. 3:13)? Are you ready to regard all you have— rank, name, talents, riches, influence, distinctions—valuable, only so far as they contribute to promote the glory of him who is first and last, and all in all?

Seek to feel that your heavenly Father's is not only a business, but the business of life. "Whose I am, and whom I serve" (Acts 27:23)—let this be the superscription written on your thoughts and deeds, your employments and enjoyments, your sleeping and waking. Be not, as the fixed stars, cold and distant; but be ever bathing in the sunshine of conscious nearness to him, who is the sun and center of all happiness and joy.

Each has some appointed work to perform, some little niche in the spiritual temple to occupy. Yours may be no splendid services, no flaming or brilliant actions to blaze and dazzle in the eye of man. It may be the quiet, unobtrusive inner work, the secret prayer, the mortified sin, the forgiven injury, the trifling act of self-sacrifice for God's glory and the good of others, of which no eye but the Eye which sees in secret is cognizant.

It matters not how small. Remember, with him, motive dignifies action. It is not what we do, but how we do it. He can be glorified in little things as well as great things, and by nothing more than the daily walk, the daily life.

Beware of any thing that would interfere with a surrender of heart and soul to his service—worldly entanglements, indulged sin, an uneven walk, a divided heart, nestling in creature comforts, shrinking from the cross.

How many hazard, if they do not make shipwreck, of their eternal hopes by becoming idlers in the vineyard—lingerers, like Lot; world-lovers, like Demas; do-nothing Christians, like the inhabitants of Meroz (see Jgs. 5:23)! The command is, "Go, work!"

Words tell what you should be; deeds tell what you are. Let those around you see there is a reality in walking with God, and working for God!

Arm yourselves likewise with the same mind!

Be Thou my vision, O Lord of my heart,
Be all else naught to me, save that Thou art;
Thou my best thought in the day and the night,
Both waking and sleeping, Thy presence my light.

— Author Unknown

- *Day 4* -
Forgiveness of Injuries

"Then said Jesus, 'Father, forgive them;
for they know not what they do.'"
Luke 23:34

Many a death struggle has been made to save a friend. A dying Savior gathers up his expiring breath to plead for his foes!

At the climax of his own woe, and of human ingratitude—man-forsaken, and God-deserted—Jesus' faltering voice mingles with the shout of his murderers, "Father, forgive them; for they know not what they do!" Had the faithless Peter been there, could he have wondered at the reply to a former question, "Lord, how often shall my brother sin against me, and I forgive him?—till seven times?" Jesus said unto him, "I say not unto thee, until seven times; but, until seventy times seven" (Mt. 18:21).

Superiority to insult and reproach, with some, proceeds from a callous and indifferent temperament, a cold, impassive, stoical insensibility, alike to kindness or unkindness. It was not so with Jesus. The tender sensibilities of his holy nature rendered him keenly sensible to ingratitude and injury, whether this was manifested in the malice of undisguised enmity, or the treachery of trusted friendship.

Perhaps to a noble nature the latter of these is the more deeply wounding. Many are inclined to forgive an open and unmasked antagonist, who are not so willing to forget or forgive heartless faithfulness, or unrequited love. But see, too, in this respect, the conduct of the blessed Redeemer! Mark how he deals with his own disciples who had basely forsaken him and fled, and that, too, in the hour he most needed their sympathy. No sooner does he rise from the dead than he hastens to disarm their fears and to assure them of an unaltered and unalterable affection. "Go tell my brethren" (Mt. 28:10), is the first message he sends; "Peace be unto you" (Jn. 20:19), is the salutation at the first meeting; "Children," (Jn. 21:5) is the word with which he first greets them on the shores of Tiberias. Even Joseph, (the Old Testament type and pattern of generous forgiveness,) when he makes himself known to his brothers, recalls the bitter thought, "Whom ye sold into Egypt" (Gen. 45:4). The true Joseph, when he reveals himself to his disciples, buries in oblivion the memory of bygone faithlessness. He meets them with a benediction. He leaves them at his ascension with the same: "he lifted up his hands and blessed them" (Lk. 24:50).

Reader, follow in all this the spirit of your Lord and Master. In rising from the study of his holy example, seek to feel that with you there shall be no such name, no such word, as enemy! Harbor no resentful thought, indulge in no bitter recrimination. Surrender yourself to no sullen fretfulness. Let "the law of kindness" (Prov. 31:26) be in your heart. Put the best construction on the failings of others; make no injurious comments on their frailties, no uncharitable insinuations. "Consider thyself, lest thou also be tempted" (Gal. 6:1).

When disposed at any time to cherish an unforgiving spirit toward a brother, think, if your God had retained his anger forever, where would you have been? If he, the Infinite One, who might have spurned you forever from his presence, has had patience with you, and forgiven you all, will you, on account of some petty grievance which your calmer moments would pronounce unworthy of a thought, indulge in the look of cold estrangement, the unrelenting word, or unforgiving deed? "If any man have a quarrel against any, even as Christ forgave you, so also do ye" (Col. 3:13).

Arm yourselves likewise with the same mind!

More like Jesus would I be,
let my Savior dwell with me;
Fill my soul with peace and love —
make me gentle as a dove.

More like Jesus, while I go,
pilgrim in this world below;
Poor in spirit would I be;
let my Savior dwell in me.

— Fanny Crosby (1820-1915)

- *Day 5* -
Meekness

"I am meek and lowly in heart."
Matthew 11:29

There is often a beautiful blending of majesty and humility, magnanimity and lowliness, in great minds.

The mightiest and holiest of all Beings that ever trod our world was the meekest of all. The Ancient of Days was as the "infant of days." He who had listened to nothing but angel melodies from all eternity, found, while on earth, melody in the lispings of an infant's voice, or in an outcast's tears!

No wonder an innocent lamb was his emblem, or that the anointing Spirit came down upon him in the form of the gentle dove. He had the wealth of worlds at his feet. The hosts of heaven had only to be summoned as his retinue. But all the pageantry of the world, all its dreams of carnal glory, had, for him, no fascination. The Tempter, from a mountain summit, showed him a wide scene of splendid misery; but he spurned alike the thought and the Adversary away! John and James would call down fire from heaven on a Samaritan village; he rebukes the vengeful suggestion! Peter, on the night of the betrayal, cuts off the ear of an assassin; the intended Victim, again, only challenges his disciple, and heals his enemy!

Arraigned before Pilate's judgment seat, how meekly he bears nameless wrongs and indignities! Suspended on the cross—the denunciations of the multitude are rising around, but he hears as though he heard them not. They extract no angry look, no bitter word—"Behold the Lamb of God!" Need we wonder that *meekness* and *poverty of spirit* should stand foremost in his own cluster of beatitudes, that he should select this among all his other qualities for the peculiar study and imitation of his disciples, "Learn of Me, for I am meek" (Mt. 11:29), or that an apostle should exhort "by the meekness and gentleness of Christ" (2 Cor. 10:1).

How different the world's maxims, and his! The world's: "Resent the affront, vindicate honor"; his: "Overcome evil with good" (Rom. 12:21). The world's: "Only let it be when for your faults ye are buffeted that ye take it patiently"; his: "When ye do well and suffer for it, ye take it patiently, this is acceptable with God." (1 Pet. 2:20).

Reader, strive to obtain, like your adorable Lord, this "ornament of a meek and quiet spirit, which, in the sight of God, is of great price" (1 Pet.3:4). Be *clothed* with gentleness and humility.

Follow not the world's fleeting shadows that mock you as you grasp them. If always aspiring—ever soaring on the wing—you are likely to become discontented, proud, selfish, time-serving. In whatever position of life God has placed you, be satisfied. What!

Are you ambitious to be on a pinnacle of the temple—a higher place in the Church, or in the world? Satan might hurl you down! "Be not high-minded, but fear" (Rom. 11:20). And with respect to others, honor their gifts, contemplate their excellences only to imitate them. Speak kindly, act gently, "condescend to men of low estate" (Rom. 12:16).

Be assured, no happiness is equal to that enjoyed by the *meek* Christian. He has within him a perpetual inner sunshine, a perennial wellspring of peace. Never ruffled and fretted by real or imagined injuries, he puts the best construction on motives and actions, and by a gentle answer to unmerited reproach often disarms wrath.

Arm yourselves likewise with the same mind!

Though heaven be high, the gate is low,
And he that comes in there must bow:
The lofty looks shall ne'er
Have entrance there.

O God! since thou delight'st to rest
In the humble contrite breast
First make me so to be,
Then dwell with me.

— Thomas Washbourne (1606-1687)

- *Day 6* -
Thankfulness

"I thank Thee, O Father, Lord of heaven and earth."
Matthew 11:25

A thankful spirit pervaded the entire life of Jesus, and surrounded with a heavenly halo his otherwise darkened path. In moments we least expect to find it, this beautiful ray breaks through the gloom. In instituting the memorial of his death, he "gave thanks" (Mt. 26:27)! Even in crossing the Kidron to Gethsemane, he sang a hymn (see Mt. 26:30).

We know in seasons of deep sorrow and trial that every thing wears a gloomy aspect. Speechless, nature herself to the burdened spirit, seems as if she partook in the hues of sadness. The life of Jesus was one continuous experience of deprivation and woe—a "Valley of Baca" (Psa. 84:6) from first to last. Yet, amid accents of plaintive sorrow, there are ever heard subdued undertones of thankfulness and joy!

Ah, if he, the suffering "man of sorrows" (Isa. 53:3) could, during a life of unparalleled woe, lift up his heart in grateful acknowledgment to his Father in heaven, how ought the lives of those to be one perpetual *hymn of thankfulness*, who are from day to day and hour to hour (for all they have, both temporally and spiritually) dependents on God's bounty and love!

Reader, cultivate this thankful spirit; it will be to you a perpetual feast. There is, or ought to be, with us no such thing as small *mercies*; all are *great*, because the least are undeserved. Indeed, a really thankful heart will extract motive for gratitude from everything, making the most even of scanty blessings. St. Paul, when in his dungeon at Rome, a prisoner in chains, is heard to say, "I have all, and abound" (Phil. 4:18).

Guard, on the other hand, against that spirit of continual fretting and moping over fancied ills; that temptation to exaggerate the real or supposed disadvantages of our condition, magnifying the trifling inconveniences of every-day life into enormous evils. Think, rather, how much we have to be thankful for.

The world in which we live, in spite of all the scars of sin and suffering upon it, is a happy world. It is not, as many would morbidly paint it, flooded with tears and strewn with wrecks, plaintive with a perpetual dirge of sorrow. True, the Everlasting Hills are in glory, but there are numberless examples of grace, and love, and mercy below. Many green spots are in the lower valley, many more than we deserve!

God will reward a thankful spirit. Just as on earth, when a man receives with gratitude what is given, we are more disposed to give again, so also, "the Lord loveth" a cheerful *receiver*, as well as a "cheerful giver" (2 Cor. 9:7).

Let ours, moreover, be a Gospel of thankfulness. Let the incense of a grateful spirit rise not only to the Great Giver of all good, but to our Covenant God in Christ. Let it be the spirit of the child exulting in the bounty and beneficence of his Father's house and home! "Giving thanks always for all things unto God and the Father, in the name of our Lord Jesus Christ" (Eph. 5:20).

While the sweet melody of gratitude vibrates through every successive moment of our daily being, let love to our adorable Redeemer show for whom and for what it is we reserve our notes of loftiest and most fervent praise. "Thanks be unto God for his unspeakable gift" (2 Cor. 9:15)!

Arm yourselves likewise with the same mind!

All praise and thanks to God the Father now be given;
The Son and Him who reigns with Them in highest Heaven;
The one eternal God, whom earth and Heaven adore;
For thus it was, is now, and shall be evermore.

— Martin Rinkart (1586-1649)

- *Day 7* -
Unselfishness

"For even Christ pleased not himself."
Romans 15:8.

Too legibly are the characters written on the fallen heart and a fallen world, "All seek their own" (Phil. 2:21)!

Selfishness is the great law of our degenerate nature. When the love of God was dethroned from the soul, self vaulted into the vacant seat, and there, in some one of its Proteus [a mythical Greek sea-god] shapes, continues to reign. Jesus stands out for our imitation a grand solitary exception in the midst of a world of selfishness. His entire life was one abnegation of self; a beautiful living embodiment of that charity which "seeketh not her own" (1 Cor. 13:5).

He who for others turned water into wine, and provided a miraculous supply for the fainting thousands in the wilderness, exerted no such miraculous power for his own necessities. During his forty days' temptation, no table did he spread for himself, no booth did he rear for his unpillowed head. Twice do we read of him shedding tears—on neither occasion were they for himself. The approach of his cross and passion, instead of absorbing him in his own approaching suffering, seemed only to elicit new and more gracious promises to his people. When his enemies came to apprehend him, his only stipulation was for his disciples' release—"Let these go their way" (Jn. 18:8). In the very act of departure, with all the boundless glories of eternity in sight, they were still all his care.

Ah, how different is the spirit of the world! With how many is day after day only a new oblation to that idol which never darkened with its shadow his holy heart; pampering their own wishes; envying and grieving at the good of a neighbor; unable to brook the praise of a rival; establishing their own reputation on the ruins of another—thus engendering jealousy, discontent, peevishness, and every kindred unholy passion. "But ye have not so learned Christ" (Eph. 4:20)!

Reader, have you been sitting at the feet of him who "pleased not himself"? Are you "dying daily" (Lk. 9:23)—dying to self as well as to sin? Are you animated with this as the high end and aim of existence—to lay out your time, and talents, and opportunities, for God's glory, and the good of your fellow-men; not seeking your own interests, but rather ceding these, if, by doing so, another will be made happier, and your Savior honored?

You may not have it in your power to manifest this "mind of Jesus" on a great scale, by enduring great sacrifices; nor is this required. His denial of self had about it no repulsive austerity. But you can evince its holy influence and sway by innumerable little acts of kindness and goodwill, taking a generous interest in the welfare and pursuits of others, or engaging and cooperating in strategies for the mitigation of human misery.

Avoid ostentation—another repulsive form of self. Be willing to be in the shade; sound no trumpet before you. The evangelist Matthew made a great feast, which was graced by the presence of Jesus. In his Gospel he says not one word about it!

Seek to live more constantly and habitually under the constraining influence of the love of Jesus. Selfishness withers and dies beneath Calvary.

Ah, believer! If Christ had "pleased himself," where would you have been this day?

Arm yourselves likewise with the same mind!

More about Jesus would I know,
More of His grace to others show;
More of His saving fullness see,
More of His love who died for me.

— Eliza E. Hewitt (1851-1920)

- *Day 8* -
Submission to God's Word

"Jesus said unto him, 'It is written . . .'"
Matthew 4:7

We can not fail to be struck, in the course of the Savior's public teaching, with his constant appeal to the Word of God.

While, at times, Jesus utters in his own name, the authoritative command, "Verily, verily, I say unto you," he as often thus introduces some mighty work, or gives intimation of some impending event in his own momentous life: "These things must come to pass" or "the Scriptures be fulfilled." He commands his people to "search the Scriptures" (Jn. 5:39), but he sets the example by searching and submitting to them himself.

Whether he drives the money changers from their sacrilegious traffic in the temple, or foils his great adversary on the mount of temptation, Jesus does so with the same weapon, "It is written." When he rises from the grave, the theme of his first discourse is one impressive tribute to the value and authority of the same sacred oracles. The disciples on the road to Emmaus listen to nothing but a Bible lesson. "He expounded unto them in all the Scriptures the things concerning himself" (Lk. 24:27).

How momentous the instruction herein conveyed! The necessity of the absolute subjection of the mind to God's written Word— making churches, creeds, ministers, books, religious opinion, all subordinate and subservient to this—"How readest thou?" (Lk. 10:26), rebuking the philosophy (falsely so called) that would distort the plain statements of Revelation, and bring them to the bar of proud reason.

If an infallible Redeemer, a law to himself, was submissive in all respects to the "written law," shall fallible man refuse to sit with the teachableness of a little child, and listen to the Divine message?

There may be, and there is, in the Bible, what reason staggers at: we have "nothing to draw with, and the well is deep" (Jn. 4:11). But, "Thus saith the Lord," is enough. Faith does not first ask what the bread is made of, but eats it. It does not analyze the components of the living stream, but with joy draws the water from "the wells of salvation" (Isa. 12:3).

Reader, take that Word as "the lamp to thy feet, and the light to thy path" (Psa. 119:105). In days when false lights are hung out, there is the more need of keeping the eye steadily fixed on the unerring beacon. Make the Bible the arbiter in all difficulties—the ultimate court of appeal. Like Mary, sit at "the feet of Jesus" (Jn. 12:3), willing only to learn of him. How many perplexities it would save you! How many fatal steps in life it would prevent—how many tears! "It is a great matter," says Thomas Chalmers (1780-1847), the noblest of modern Christian philosophers, "when the mind dwells on any passage of Scripture, just to think how true it is" (*Memoirs of the Life and Writings of Thomas Chalmers*, Vol. 3, by William Hanna, p. 145).

In every dubious question, when the foot is trembling on debatable ground, knowing not whether to advance or recede, make this the final criterion, "What saith the Scripture?" The world may remonstrate, erring friends may disapprove, Satan may tempt, ingenious arguments may explain away—but, with our finger on the revealed page, let the words of our Great Example be ever a Divine formula for our guidance: "This commandment have I received of my Father" (Jn. 10:18).

Arm yourselves likewise with the same mind!

And though this world, with devils filled, should threaten to undo us,
We will not fear, for God hath willed His truth to triumph through us:
The Prince of Darkness grim, we tremble not for him;
His rage we can endure, for lo, his doom is sure,
One little word shall fell him.

That word above all earthly powers, no thanks to them, abideth;
The Spirit and the gifts are ours through Him Who with us sideth:
Let goods and kindred go, this mortal life also;
The body they may kill: God's truth abideth still,
His kingdom is forever.

— Martin Luther (1483-1546)

- *Day 9* -
Prayerfulness

"He continued all night in prayer to God."
Luke 6:12

We speak of this Christian and that Christian as "a man of prayer." Jesus was emphatically so. The Spirit was poured upon him without "measure" (see Jn. 3:34) yet—he prayed!

He was incarnate wisdom, needing not that any should teach him. He was infinite in his power, and boundless in his resources, yet— he prayed! How deeply sacred the prayerful memories that hover around the solitudes of Olivet and the shores of Tiberias! He seemed often to turn night into day to redeem moments for prayer, rather than lose the blessed privilege.

We are rarely, indeed, admitted into the solemnities of his inner life. The veil of night is generally between us and the Great High Priest, when he entered the holiest of all; but we have enough to reveal the depth and fervor, the tenderness and confidentiality of this blissful intercommunion with his heavenly Father. No morning dawns without his fetching fresh manna from the mercy seat. "He wakeneth morning by morning; he wakeneth mine ear to hear as the learned" (Isa. 50:4). Beautiful description! A praying Redeemer, wakening, as if at early dawn, the ear of his Father, to get fresh supplies for the duties and the trials of the day! All his public acts were consecrated by prayer—his baptism, his transfiguration, his miracles, his agony, his death. He breathed away his spirit in prayer. "His last breath," says Philip Henry (1631-1696), "was praying breath."

How sweet to think, in holding communion with God—Jesus drank of this very brook! He consecrated the bended knee and the silent closet. He refreshed his fainting spirit at the same great Fountainhead from which it is life for us to draw and death to forsake.

Reader, do you complain of your languid spirit, your drooping faith, your fitful affections, your lukewarm love? May you not trace much of what you deplore to an unfrequented prayer closet? The treasures are locked up from you, because you have suffered the key to rust; the hands hang down because they have ceased to be uplifted in prayer. Without prayer—it is the pilgrim without a staff, the seaman without a compass, the soldier going unarmed and unharnessed to battle.

Beware of encouraging what disinclines to prayer—going to the prayer closet with soiled garments, the din of the world following you, its distracting thoughts hovering unforbidden over your spirit. Can you wonder that the living water refuses to flow through obstructed channels, or the heavenly light to pierce murky vapors!

On earth, fellowship with a lofty order of minds imparts a certain nobility to the character; so, in a far higher sense, by communion with God you will be transformed into his image, and get assimilated to his likeness. Make every event in life a reason for fresh going to him. If duty be difficult, bring it to the test of prayer. If bowed down with anticipated trial—"fearing to enter the cloud,"—remember Christ's preparation, "Sit ye here while I go and pray yonder" (Mt. 26:312).

Let prayer consecrate every thing—your time, talents, pursuits, engagements, joys, sorrows, crosses, losses. By it, rough paths will be made smooth, trials disarmed of their bitterness, enjoyments hallowed and refined, the bread of the world turned into angels' food. "It is in the closet," says Edward Payson (1783-1827), "the battle is lost or won!"

Arm yourselves likewise with the same mind!

O Thou by Whom we come to God,
The Life, the Truth, the Way,
The path of prayer Thyself hast trod:
Lord, teach us how to pray.
— James Montgomery (1771-1854)

- Day 10 -
Love to the Brothers

"And walk in love, as Christ also hath loved us."
Ephesians 5:2

"Jesus," says a writer, "came from heaven on the wings of love." It was the element in which he moved and walked. He sought to baptize the world afresh with it. When we find him teaching us by love to vanquish an enemy, we need not wonder at the tenderness of his appeals to the brothers to "love one another." Like a fond father impressing his children, how the Divine Teacher lingers over the lesson, "This is My commandment" (Jn. 15:12).

If selfishness had guided Jesus' actions, we might have expected him to demand all his people's love for himself. But he claims no such monopoly. He not only encourages mutual affection, but he makes it the badge of discipleship! He gives them at once its measure and motive. "Love one another, as I have loved you!" What a love was that! It reached to the lowliest and humblest: "Inasmuch as ye did it to the least of these, ye did it unto Me" (Mt. 25:40).

Ah! if such was the Elder Brother's love to his younger brothers, what should the love of these younger brothers be for one another! How humbling that there should be so much that is sadly and strangely unlike the spirit which our blessed Master sought to inculcate alike by precept and example! Christians, why these bitter estrangements, these censorious words, these harsh judgments, this lack of kind consideration of the feelings and failings of those who may differ from you? Why are your friendships so often like the summer brook, soon dried? You hope, before long, to meet in glory. Doubtless when you enter on that Sabbath of Love, many a greeting will be this, "Alas! my brother, that on earth I did not love you more!"

Do you see the image of God in a professing believer? It is your duty to love him for the sake of that image. No church, no outward garment, no denominational creed, should prevent your owning and claiming him as a fellow-pilgrim and fellow-heir. It has been said of a portrait, however poor the painting, however unfinished the style, however faulty the touches, however coarse and unseemly the frame, yet if the likeness be faithful, we overlook many lesser defects. So it is with the Christian. However plain the exterior, however rough the setting, or even manifold the blemishes still found clinging to a partially sanctified nature, yet if the Redeemer's likeness be feebly and faintly traced there, we should love the copy for the sake of the Divine Original.

There may be other bonds of association and communion linking spirit with spirit: family ties, mental pleasantries, intellectual tastes, benevolent pursuits—but that which ought to take the precedence of all, is the love of God's image in the brothers. What will heaven be but this love perfected—loving Christ, and beloved by those who love him?

Reader, seek to love him more, and you will love his people more. John had more love than the other disciples. Why? He drank deepest of the love within that bosom on which he delighted to lean, every beat of which was love. "Walk," then, "in love" (Eph. 5:2). Let it be the very foot-road you tread; let your way to heaven be paved with it. Soon shall we come to look within the portal. Then shall every jarring and dissonant note be merged into the sublime harmonies of "the new heavens and the new earth" (Isa. 65:17), and we shall all *see eye to eye*!

Arm yourselves likewise with the same mind!

I love Thee so I know not how
My transports to control;
Thy love is like a burning fire
Within my very soul.

Burn, burn, O love, within my heart,
Burn fiercely night and day,
Till all the dross of earthly loves
Is burned, and burned away.

— Frederick W. Faber (1814-1863)

- *Day 11* -
Sympathy

"Jesus wept."
John 11:35

It is an affecting thing to see a great Man in tears! "Jesus wept!" It was ever his delight to tread in the footsteps of sorrow—to heal the broken-hearted—turning aside from his own path of suffering to "weep with those that weep" (Rom. 12:15).

Bethany! That scene, that word, is a condensed volume of consolation for yearning and desolate hearts. What a majesty in those tears! He had just been discoursing on himself as the Resurrection and the Life—the next moment he is a Weeping Man by a human grave, melted in anguished sorrow at a bereaved one's side! Think of the funeral at the gate of Nain, reading its lesson to dejected myriads—"Let thy widows trust in me" (Jer. 49:11). Think of the farewell discourse to his disciples, when, muffling all his own foreseen and anticipated sorrows, he thought only of soothing and mitigating theirs! Think of the affecting pause in that silent procession to Calvary, when he turns round and stills the sobs of those who are tracking his steps with their weeping! Think of that wondrous epitome of human tenderness, just ere his eyes closed in their sleep of agony—in the mightiest crisis of all time—when filial love looked down on an anguished mother, and provided her a son and a home!

Ah, was there ever sympathy like this—Son! Brother! Kinsman! Savior! all in one! The majesty of Godhead almost lost in the tenderness of a Friend. But so it was, and so it is. The heart of the now enthroned King beats responsive to the humblest of his sorrow-stricken people. "I am poor and needy, yet the Lord carries me on his heart" (Psa. 40:17). Let us *go and do likewise*. Let us be ready, like our Lord, to follow the beck of misery—"to deliver the needy when he crieth, the poor also, and him that hath no helper" (Psa. 72:12).

Sympathy costs but little. Its recompense and return are great, in the priceless consolation it imparts. Few there are who undervalue it. Look at Paul—the weary, jaded prisoner—chained to a soldier—recently wrecked, about to stand before Caesar. He reaches Appii Forum and the Three Taverns, dejected and depressed. Brethren come from Rome, a distance of sixty miles, to offer their sympathy. The aged man is cheered! His spirit, like Jacob's, "revived!" "He thanked God, and took courage" (see Acts 28:14-15).

Reader, let *this mind*, this holy, Christ-like habit be in you, which was also in your adorable Master. Delight, when opportunity occurs, to frequent the house of mourning—to bind up the widow's heart, and to dry the orphan's tears. If you can do nothing else, you can whisper into the ear of disconsolate sorrow those majestic solaces, which, rising first in the graveyard of Bethany, have sent their undying echoes through the world, and stirred the depths of ten thousand hearts. "Exercise your souls," says Joseph Butler (1692-1752), "in a loving sympathy with sorrow in every form. Soothe it, minister to it, succor it, revere it. It is the relic of Christ in the world, an image of the Great Sufferer, a shadow of the cross. It is a holy and venerable thing."

Jesus himself "looked for some to take pity, but there was none; and for comforters, but he found none" (Psa. 69:20). It shows how even he valued sympathy, and that, too, in its commonest form of "pity," though an ungrateful world denied it.

Arm yourselves likewise with the same mind!

Before our Father's throne
We pour our ardent prayers;
Our fears, our hopes, our aims are one
Our comforts and our cares.

We share each other's woes,
Our mutual burdens bear;
And often for each other flows
The sympathizing tear.

— John Fawcett (1740-1817)

- *Day 12* -
Fidelity in Rebuke

"The Lord turned and looked upon Peter."
Luke 22:61

Jesus never spoke one unnecessarily harsh or severe word. He had a Divine sympathy for the frailties and infirmities of a tried, and suffering, and tempted nature in others. He was forbearing to the ignorant, encouraging to the weak, tender to the penitent, loving to all, —yet how faithful was he as "the Reprover of sin" (see Ezek. 3:26).

Silent under his own wrongs, with what burning invectives did Jesus lay bare the Pharisees' masked corruption and hypocrisy! When his Father's name and temple were profaned, how did he sweep, with an avenging hand, the mammon-crowd away, replacing the superscription, "Holiness to the Lord," over the defiled altars!

Nor was it different with his own disciples. With what fidelity, when rebuke was needed, did he administer it: the withering reprimand conveyed sometimes by an impressive word (see Mt. 16:23); sometimes by a silent look (see Luke 22:61). "Faithful always were the wounds of this Friend" (Prov. 27:6).

Reader, are you equally faithful with your Lord in rebuking evil; not with "the wrath of man, which worketh not the righteousness of God" (Jas. 1:20), but with a holy jealousy of his glory, feeling, with the sensitive honor of "the good soldier of Jesus Christ" (2 Tim. 2:3), that an affront offered to him is offered to yourself?

The giving of a wise reproof requires much Christian prudence and delicate discretion. It is not by a rash and inconsiderate exposure of failings that we must attempt to reclaim an erring brother. But neither, for the sake of a false peace, must we compromise fidelity; even friendship is too dearly purchased by winking at sin. Perhaps, when Peter was led to call the apostle who honestly reproved him, "Our beloved brother Paul" (2 Pet. 3:15), in nothing did he love his rebuker more, than for the honest boldness of his Christian reproof. If Paul had, in that crisis of the Church, with a timidity unworthy of him, evaded the ungracious task, what, humanly speaking, might have been the result (see Gal. 2:11f)?

How often does a seasonable reprimand, a faithful caution, save a lifetime of sin and sorrow! How many a death bed has made the disclosure, "That kind warning of my friend put an arrest on my career of guilt; it altered my whole being; it brought me to the cross, touched my heart, and, by God's grace, saved my soul!" On the other hand, how many have felt, when death has put his impressive seal on some close earthly intimacy, "To this friend, or that friend—I might have spoken a solemn word to him; but now he is no more; the opportunity is lost, never to be recalled!"

Reader, see that you act not the spiritual coward. When tempted to sit silent when the name of God is slighted or dishonored, think, would Jesus have done so? Would he have allowed the oath to go unrebuked, the lie to be uttered unchallenged, the Sabbath with impunity to be profaned? Where there is a natural diffidence which makes you shrink from a more bold and open reproof, remember much may be done to discountenance sin by the silent holiness of demeanor which refuses to smile at the unholy allusion or ribald jest.

"A word spoken in due season, how good is it" (Prov. 15:23). Speak *gently*, yet speak faithfully: "be pitiful, be courteous" (1 Pet. 3:8), yet "quit [act] you like men, be strong" (1 Cor. 16:13).

Arm yourselves likewise with the same mind!

Pity from Thine eye let fall,
By a look my soul recall;
Now the stone to flesh convert,
Cast a look, and break my heart.

Now incline me to repent,
Let me now my sins lament,
Now my foul revolt deplore,
Weep, believe, and sin no more.

— Charles Wesley (1707-1788)

- *Day 13* -
Gentleness in Rebuke

"Simon, son of Jonas, lovest thou me?"
John 21:15

No word here of the erring disciple's past faithlessness—his guilty cowardice, unmentioned; his base denial—his oaths and curses, and treacherous desertion, all unmentioned! The memory of a threefold denial is suggested, and no more, by the threefold question of unutterable tenderness, "Simon, son of Jonas, lovest thou me?"

When Jesus finds his disciples sleeping at the gate of Gethsemane, he rebukes them; but how is the rebuke disarmed of its poignancy by the merciful apology which is added: "The spirit indeed is willing, but the flesh is weak" (Mt. 26:41). How different from their unkind insinuation regarding him, when, in the vessel on Tiberias, "he was asleep"—"Master carest thou not that we perish?" (Mk. 4:38). The woman of Samaria is full of earthliness, carnality, sectarianism, guilt. Yet how gently the Savior speaks to her—how forbearingly, yet faithfully. He directs the arrow of conviction to that seared and hardened conscience, till he lays it bleeding at his feet! Truly, "he will not break the bruised reed; he will not quench the smoking flax" (Isa. 42:3). By "the goodness of God" (Rom. 2:4) he would lead to repentance. When others are speaking of merciless violence, he can dismiss the most guilty of profligates with the words, "Neither do I condemn thee; go, and sin no more" (Jn. 8:11).

How many have an unholy pleasure in finding a brother in the wrong—blazing abroad his failings, administering rebuke, not in gentle forbearance and kindly expostulation, but with harsh and impatient severity! How beautifully did Jesus unite intense sensibility to sin, along with tenderest compassion for the sinner, showing in this that "he knoweth our frame" (Psa. 103:14).

Many a scholar needs gentleness in chastisement. The reverse would crush a sensitive spirit, or drive it to despair. Jesus tenderly *considers* the case of those he disciplines, "tempering the wind to the shorn lamb." In the picture of the good shepherd bearing home the wandering sheep, he illustrated by parable what he had often and again taught by his own example. No word of needless harshness or upbraiding uttered to the erring wanderer! Ingratitude is too deeply felt to need rebuke! In silent love, "he lays it on his shoulders rejoicing" (Lk. 15:5).

Reader, seek to mingle gentleness in all your rebukes; bear with the infirmities of others; make allowance for constitutional frailties; never say harsh things, if kind things will do as well; do not unnecessarily lacerate with recalling former delinquencies. In reproving another, let us rather feel how much we need reproof ourselves. "Consider thyself" (Gal. 6:1) is a searching Scripture motto for dealing with an erring brother. Remember your Lord's method of silencing fierce accusation—"Let him that is without sin cast the first stone" (Jn. 8:7).

Moreover, anger and severity are not the successful means of re-claiming the backslider, or of melting the obdurate. Like the smooth stones with which David smote Goliath, gentle rebukes are generally the most powerful. The old fable of the traveler and his cloak has a moral here as in other things. The genial sunshine will effect its removal sooner than the rough tempest. It was said of Robert Leighton (1611-1684), that "he rebuked faults so mildly, that they were never repeated, not because the admonished were afraid, but ashamed to do so."

Arm yourselves likewise with the same mind!

Kind words toward those you daily meet.
Kind words and actions right,
Will make this life of ours most sweet,
Turn darkness into light.
— Isaac Watts (1674-1748)

- *Day 14* -
Endurance in Contradiction

"Who endured such contradiction of sinners against himself."
Hebrews 12:3

What endurance was this! Perfect truth in the midst of error; perfect love in the midst of ingratitude and coldness; perfect rectitude in the midst of perjury, violence, fraud; perfect constancy in the midst of harsh language and desertion; perfect innocence, confronting every debased form of depravity and guilt; perfect patience, encountering every kind of gross provocation—"oppressed and afflicted, he opened not his mouth" (Isa. 53:7) "For my love" (in return for my love), "they are mine adversaries" (Psa. 38:20), but (see his endurance, the only kind of revenge of which his sinless nature was capable) "I give myself unto prayer!" (Psa. 109:4).

Reader, "let this mind be in you, which was also in Christ Jesus!" The greatest test of an earthly soldier's courage is patient endurance! The noblest trait of the spiritual soldier is the same. "Having done all to stand" (Eph. 6:13), "he endured, as seeing him who is invisible" (Heb. 6:15).

Beware of the angry recrimination, the hasty outburst of temper. Amid unkind insinuations—when motives are misrepresented, and reputation assailed; when good deeds are ridiculed, kind intentions coldly thwarted and repulsed, chilling reserve manifested where you expected nothing but friendship—what a triumph over natural impulse to manifest a spirit of meek endurance, like a rainbow, radiant with the hues of heaven, resting peacefully amid the storms of derision and "the floods of ungodly men" (Psa. 18:4). What an opportunity of magnifying the *sustaining* grace of God! "It is a small thing for me to be judged of you, or of man's judgment; he that judgeth me is the Lord" (1 Cor. 4:3). "The Lord is on my side; I will not fear what man can do unto me" (Psa. 118.6). "Blessed is the man that endureth" (Jas. 1:12). "He that endureth to the end, the same shall be saved" (Mt. 10:22).

If faithful to our God, we must expect to encounter contradiction in the same form which Jesus did—"the contradiction of sinners." It has been well said, "There is no cross of nails and wood erected now for the Christian, but there is one of words and looks which is never taken down." If believers are set as lights in the earth, lamps in the *city of destruction*, we know that "he that doeth evil hateth the light" (Jn. 3:20). "Marvel not, my brethren, if the world hate you" (1 Jn. 3:13).

Weary and faint ones, exposed to the shafts of slander and scorn because of your fidelity to your God; encountering, it may be, the coldness and estrangement of those dear to you, who can not, perhaps, sympathize in the holiness of your walk and the loftiness of your aims, "consider him that endured such contradiction of sinners against himself, lest ye be weary and faint in your minds!"

What is your "contradiction" to Jesus'? Soon your cross, whatever it be, will have an end. The seat of the scorner has no place in yonder glorious heaven, where all will be peace—no jarring note to disturb its blissful harmonies! Look forward to the great coronation day of the Church triumphant—the day of your divine Lord's appearing, when motives and aims, now misunderstood, will be vindicated, wrongs redressed, slanders and aspersions wiped away.

Meanwhile, "rejoice that you are counted worthy to suffer shame for his name" (Acts 5:41).

Arm yourselves likewise with the same mind!

There are briars besetting every path,
That call for patient care;
There is a cross in every lot,
And an earnest need for prayer;
But a lowly heart, that leans on Thee
Is happy anywhere.

— Anna L. Waring (1823-1910)

- *Day 15* -
Pleasing God

"I do always those things that please him."
John 8:29

What a glorious motto for a man—"I live for God!" It is religion's truest definition. It is the essence of angelic bliss—the motive-principle of angelic action: "Ye ministers of his, that do his pleasure" (Psa. 103:21). The Lord of angels knew no higher, no other motive. It was, during his incarnation, the regulator and directory of his daily being. It supported him amid the depressing sorrows of his woe-worn path. It upheld him in their awful termination in the garden and on the cross. For a moment, sinking human nature faltered under the load his Godhead sustained; but the thought of "pleasing God" nerved and revived him. "Not my will, but Thine be done" (Lk. 22:42).

It is only when the love of God is shed abroad in the heart, that this animating desire to "please him" can exist. In the holy bosom of Jesus, that love reigned paramount, admitting no rival—no competing affection. Though infinitely inferior in degree, it is the same impelling principle which leads his people still to link enjoyment with his service, and which makes consecration to him of heart and life its own best recompense and reward.

"There is a gravitation," says the biographer of William Hewiston (1812-1850)—whose life was the holy echo of his words—"in the moral as in the physical world. When love to God is habitually in the ascendant, or occupying the place of will, it gathers round it all the other desires of the soul as satellites, and whirls them along with it in its orbit round the center of attraction." Till the heart, then, be changed, the believer cannot have "this testimony that he pleases God" (Heb. 11:5). The world, self, sin—these be the gods of the unregenerate soul. And even when changed, alas that there should be so many ebbings and flowings in our tide of devotion! Jesus could say, "I do always those things that please the Father." Glory to God burned within his bosom like a living fire. "Many waters could not quench it" (Sg. 8:7). His were no fitful and inconsistent frames and feelings, but the persistent habit of a holy life, which had the one end in view, from which it never diverged or deviated.

Let it be so, in some lowly measure with us. Let God's service not be the mere garment of high days—of set times and seasons; but, like the alabaster box of ointment, let us ever be giving forth the fragrant perfume of holiness. Even when the shadows of trial are falling around us, let us pass through the *cloud* with the sustaining motive—"All my wish, O God, is to please and glorify Thee! By giving or taking, by smiting or healing, by the sweet cup or the bitter—'Father, glorify thy name!'" "I don't want to be weary of God's dealing with me," said Edward Bickersteth (1825-1906), on his death-bed. "I want to glorify Jesus in them, and to find him more precious."

Do I shrink from trials, duties, crosses, because involving hardships and self-denial, or because frowned on by the world? Let the thought of God's approving countenance be enough. Let me dread no censure, if conscious of acting in accordance with his will. Let the apostle's warning word determine many a perplexing path: "If I please men, I am not the servant of Christ" (Gal. 1:10).

Arm yourselves likewise with the same mind!

O Lord, my best desire fulfil,
And help me to resign
Life, health, and comfort to thy will,
And make thy pleasure mine.

Why should I shrink at thy command,
Whose love forbids my fears?
Or tremble at the gracious hand
That wipes away my tears?

— William Cowper (1731-1800)

- *Day 16* -
Grief at Sin

"Being grieved for the hardness of their hearts."
Mark 3:5

On this one occasion only is the expression used with reference to Jesus—(what intensity of emotion does it denote, spoken of a sinless nature!)—"he looked round on them with anger!" Never did he grieve for himself. His most intense sorrows were reserved for those who were tampering with their own souls, and dishonoring his God. The continual spectacle of moral evil, thrust on the gaze of spotless purity, made his earthly history one consecutive history of grief, one perpetual *cross and passion*.

In the tears shed at the grave of Bethany, sympathy, doubtless, for the world's myriad mourners, had its own share (the bereaved could not part with so precious a tribute in their hours of sadness), but a far more impressive cause was one undiscerned by the weeping sisters and sorrowing crowd; his knowledge of the deep and obdurate impenitence of those who were about to gaze on the mightiest of miracles, only to "despise, and wonder, and perish" (acts 13:412). "Jesus wept!"—but his profoundest anguish was over resisted grace, abused privileges, scorned mercy. It was the Divine Artificer mourning over his shattered handiwork; the Almighty Creator weeping over his ruined world; God, the God-man, *grieving* over the temple of the soul, a humiliating wreck of what once was made *after his own image*!

Can we sympathize in any respect with such exalted tears? Do we mourn for sin, our own sin—the deep insult which it inflicts on God—the ruinous consequences it entails on ourselves? Do we grieve at sin in others? Do we know anything of "vexing our souls," like righteous Lot, "from day to day" (2 Pet. 2:8), with the world's "unlawful deeds," the stupid hardness and obduracy of the depraved heart, which resists alike the applications of wrath and love, judgment and mercy? Ah! it is easy, in general terms, to condemn vice, and to utter harsh, severe, and cutting denunciations on the guilty. It is easy to pass uncharitable comments on the inconsistencies or follies of others. But to *grieve* as our Lord did, is a different thing. To mourn over the hardness of heart, and yet to have the burning desire to teach it better things; to hate, as he did, the sin, but, like him also, to love the sinner!

Reader, look especially to your own spirit. In one respect, the example of Jesus falls short of your case. He had no sin of his own to mourn over. He could only commiserate with others. Your most intense grief must begin with yourself. Like the watchful Levite of old, be a guardian at the temple gates of your own soul. Whatever be your besetting iniquity, your constitutional bias to sin, seek to guard it with wakeful vigilance. Grieve at the thought of incurring one passing shadow of displeasure from so kind and compassionate a Savior. Let this be a holy preservative in your every hour of temptation, "How can I do this great wickedness, and sin against God?" (Gen. 39:9).

Grieve for a perishing world—a groaning creation fettered and chained in unwilling "subjection to vanity" (Rom. 8:20). Do what you can, by effort, by prayer, to hasten on the hour of jubilee, when its ashy robes of sin and sorrow shall be laid aside, and, attired in the beauties of holiness, it shall exult in "the glorious liberty of the sons of God" (Rom. 8:21).

Arm yourselves likewise with the same mind!

My sins, though great, do not surpass
The power and glory of Thy grace:
Great God, Thy nature hath no bound,
So let Thy pardoning love be found.

O wash my soul from every sin,
And make my guilty conscience clean!
Here, on my heart, the burden lies,
And past offences pain my eyes.

— Isaac Watts (1674-1748)

- *Day 17* -
Humility

*"He riseth from supper, and laid aside his garments; and
took a towel, and girded himself. After that he poureth water
into a basin, and began to wash the disciples' feet . . ."*
John 13:4-5

What a matchless picture of humility! At the very moment when his
throne was in view, angel anthems floating in his ear, the hour
comes "when he was to depart out of this world" (Jn. 13:1)—
possessing a lofty consciousness of his peerless dignity, that "he
came from God and went to God (Jn. 13:3)—then "Jesus took a
towel, and girded himself, and began to wash the disciples' feet!"
All heaven was ready at that moment to cast their combined crowns
at his feet. But the High and the Lofty One, inhabiting eternity, is
on earth as one who *serves*! "That infinite stoop! It sinks all creature humiliation to nothing, and renders it impossible for a creature
to humble himself" (David Evans, 1750-1808).

Humility follows him, from his unhonored birthplace to his bor-
rowed grave. It throws a subdued splendor over all he did. "The
poor in spirit," the "mourner," the "meek," claim his first beatitudes

(see Mt. 5:3-5). He was severe only to one class—those who looked down upon others. However he is employed—whether performing his works of miraculous power, or receiving angel visitants, or taking little children in his arms, he stands forth *clothed* with humility. Nay, this humility becomes more conspicuous as he draws nearer glory. Before his death, he calls his disciples "friends;" subsequently, it is "brethren," "children" (see Jn. 15:4, 20:17, 21:5). How sad the contrast between the Master and his disciples! Two hours had not elapsed after he washed their feet, when "there was a strife among them who should be the greatest" (Lk. 22:24).

Let the mental image of that lowly Redeemer be ever bending over us. His example may well speak in silent impressiveness, bringing us down from our pedestal of pride. There surely can be no labor of love too humiliating when he stooped so low. Let us be content to take the humblest place; not envious of the success or exaltation of another; not, "like Diotrephes, loving preeminence" (3 Jn. 1:9); but willing to be thought little of; saying with the Baptist, with our eye on our Lord, "he must increase, but I must decrease" (Jn. 3:30).

How much we have cause to be humble for—the constant cleaving of defilement to our souls; and even what is partially good in us, how mixed with imperfection, self-seeking, arrogance, vain-glory! A proud Christian is a contradiction in terms. The seraphim of old (type of the Christian Church, and of believers) had six wings—two were for errands of love, but "with four he covered himself" (see Isa. 6:2)! It has been beautifully said, "You lie nearest the River of Life when you bend to it; you can not drink, but as you stoop." The corn of the field, as it ripens, bows its head; so the Christian, as he ripens in the Divine life, bends in this lowly grace. Christ speaks of his people as "lilies"—they are "lilies of the valley," they can only grow in the shade!

"Humble yourselves under the mighty hand of God" (1 Pet. 5:6). Go with what Samuel Rutherford (1600-1661) calls "a low sail." It is the garment of your blessed Master, the family badge, the family likeness. "With this man will I dwell, even with him that is humble" (Isa. 57:15). Yes! the humble, sanctified heart is God's second heaven!

Arm yourselves likewise with the same mind!

—⁂—

Search me, O God, and know my heart today;
Try me, O Savior, know my thoughts, I pray.
See if there be some wicked way in me;
Cleanse me from every sin and set me free.

— J. Edwin Orr (1912-1987)

- *Day 18* -
Patience

"He is brought as a lamb to the slaughter."
Isaiah 53:7

How great was the patience of Jesus! Even among his own disciples, how forbearingly he endured their blindness, their misconceptions and hardness of heart! Philip had been for three years with him, yet he had not *known* him—all that time he had remained in strange and culpable ignorance of his Lord's dignity and glory. See how tenderly Jesus bears with him, giving him nothing in reply for his confession of ignorance but unparalleled promises of grace! Peter, the honored and trusted, becomes a renegade and a coward. Justly might his dishonored Lord, stung with such unrequited love, have cut the unworthy hindrance down. But he spares him, bears with him, gently rebukes him, and loves him more than ever!

See the Divine Sufferer in the terminating scenes of his own ignominy and woe. How patient!—"As a sheep before her shearers is dumb, so he opened not his mouth" (Isa. 53:7). In these awful moments, outraged Omnipotence might have summoned twelve legions of angels and put into the hand of each a vial of wrath. But he submits in meek, majestic silence. Verily, in him "patience had her perfect work" (see Jas. 1:4).

Think of this same patience with his Church and people since he ascended to glory. The years upon years he has borne with their perverse resistance of his grace, their treacherous ingratitude, their wayward wanderings, their hardness of heart and contempt of his holy word. Yet, behold the forbearing love of this Savior of God! His hand of mercy is "stretched out still" (Isa. 5:25; 9:12, 17, 21; 10:4).

Child of God, are you now undergoing some bitter trial? The way of your God, it may be, is all mystery; no footprints of love traceable in the checkered path; no light in the clouds above; no ray in the dark future. Be patient! "The Lord is good to them that wait for him" (Lam. 3:25). "They that wait on the Lord shall renew their strength" (Isa. 40:31). Or have you been long tossed on some bed of sickness—days of pain and nights of weariness appointed to you? Be patient! "I trust this groaning," said a suffering saint, "is not murmuring." God, by this very affliction, is nurturing within you this beautiful grace which shone so conspicuously in the character of your dear Lord. With him it was a lovely habit of the soul. With you, the "tribulation" which works "patience" (Jas. 1:3) is needful discipline. It is good for a man that he should both hope and quietly wait for the salvation of God.

Are you suffering some unmerited wrong or unkindness, exposed to harsh and wounding accusations, hard for flesh and blood to bear? Be patient! Beware of hastiness of speech or temper; remember how much evil may be done by a few inconsiderate words spoken unadvisedly with the lip. Think of Jesus standing before a human tribunal, in the silent submissiveness of conscious innocence and integrity. Leave your cause with God. Let this be the only form of your complaint, "O God, I am oppressed; undertake Thou for me!"

"In patience," then, "possess ye your souls" (Lk. 21:19). Let it not be a grace for peculiar seasons, called forth on peculiar exigencies; but a habitual frame of mind manifested in the calm serenity of a daily walk—placidity amid the little fretting annoyances of everyday life—a fixed purpose of the heart to wait upon God, and cast its every burden upon him.

Arm yourselves likewise with the same mind!

Ye who the name of Jesus bear,
His sacred steps pursue;
And let that mind which was in Him
Be also found in you.

Though in the form of God He was,
His only Son declared,
Nor to be equally adored
As robbery did regard.

— Author Unknown

- *Day 19* -
Subjection

"As the Father gave me commandment, even so I do."
John 14:31

Jesus as the God-man had omnipotence slumbering in his arms. He had the hoarded treasures of eternity in his grasp. He had only to *speak*, and it was done. But, as an example to his people, his whole life on earth was one impressive act of subordination and dependence. At Nazareth he was "subject to his parents" (Lk. 2:51). There he remained in studied obscurity, occupying for thirty years a lowly dwelling, willing to continue in a state of seclusion, till the Father's summons called him to his appointed work.

At his baptism, sinless himself, he gives this reason for receiving a sinner's rite at a sinner's hands—"Suffer it to be so now, for thus it becometh Me to fulfill all righteousness" (Mt. 3:15). The same beautiful spirit of filial subjection shines conspicuous amid his acts of stupendous power. "Jesus lifted up his eyes and said, Father, I thank Thee that Thou hast heard Me; and I know that Thou hearest Me always; but because of the people which stand by, I said it, that they may believe that Thou has sent Me" (Jn. 11:41-42). Even among his own disciples his language is, "I am among you as he that serveth" (Lk. 22:27). With an act of submission he closed his pilgrimage and work of love. "Father, into Thy hands I commend My spirit" (Lk. 23:46).

What an example to us, in all this, is our beloved Lord! Surely, if he, "God only wise" (1 Tim. 1:17)—the Self-existent One, to whom "all power was committed" (Mt. 28:18)—the Sinless One, never liable to err, on whom "the Spirit was poured without measure" (Jn. 3:34)—if he manifested such habitual dependence on his heavenly Father, how earnestly ought we, weak, erring, fallible creatures, to seek to live every hour—every moment—as dependents on God's grace and love, following in all things his directing hand! As the servant has his eyes on his master, or the child on its parent, so should our *eyes* be on the Lord our God. However he speaks, be it ours with all docility to follow the voice, endorsing every utterance of providence, and every precept of Scripture, with our Lord's own words, "This is the Father's will!"

Beware of self-dependence. The first step in spiritual declension is this: "Let him that thinketh he standeth" (1 Cor. 10:12)! The secret of real strength is this: "Kept by the power of God" (1 Pet. 1:5)! How it sweetens all our blessings, and alleviates all our sorrows, to regard both as emanations from a loving Father's hand. Even if we should be, like the disciples of old, "constrained" to go into the ship; if all should be darkness and tempest, frowning providences— "the wind contrary" (Mt. 14:24)—how blessed to feel that in embarking on the unquiet element, "the Lord has bidden us!" Paul could not speak even of taking an earthly journey, without the parenthesis, "if the Lord will" (1Cor. 4:19). How many trials, and sorrows, and sins, would it save us, if the same were the habitual regulator of our daily life! It would lead to calm contentment with our lot, hushing every disquieting suggestion with the thought that that lot, with all that is apparently adverse in it, was ordained for us. It would teach us not to be aspiring after great things, but humbly to wait the will and purposes of a wise Provider; not to go before our heavenly Guide, but to follow him, saying, in meek subjection, "Lord, my heart is not haughty, nor mine eyes lofty, neither do I exercise myself in great matters, or in things too high for me. Surely I have behaved and quieted myself, as a child that is weaned of his mother: my soul is even as a weaned child (Psa. 131:1-2).

Arm yourselves likewise with the same mind!

Whatever dims thy sense of truth
Or stains thy purity,
Though light as breath of summer air,
O count it sin to thee.

Preserve the tablet of thy thoughts
From every blemish free,
For our Redeemer's holy faith
Its temple makes with thee.

— Mary W. Hale (1810-1862)

- *Day 20* -
Not Retaliating

"Who, when he was reviled, reviled not again."
1 Peter 2:23

What a common dictate of the fallen and regenerate heart to resent and recriminate! How alien to natural feeling to answer cutting taunts, and meet unmerited wrong with the Divine method the Gospel prescribes—"Overcome evil with good" (Rom. 12:21). It was in the closing scenes of the Savior's humiliation, when, silent and unresenting, he stood "dumb before his shearers" (Isa. 53:7), that this beautiful feature in his character was most wondrously manifested. But it beams forth, also, for our imitation in the ordinary and less prominent incidents of his pilgrimage.

When he met Nathanael of Cana in Galilee, he found him clinging to an unreasonable prejudice—"Can any good thing come out of Nazareth?" (Jn. 1:46). The severe remark is allowed to pass unnoticed. Overlooking the unkind insinuation, the Savior fixes on the favorable feature of his character, "Behold an Israelite indeed, in whom is no guile!" (Jn. 1:47). After his resurrection, he appears to his disciples. They were cowering in shame, half afraid to confront the glance of injured goodness. He breathes on them, and says, "Peace be unto you" (Jn. 20:19). Peter was the one of all the rest who had most reason to dread estranged looks and upbraiding words. But a special message is sent to reassure that trembling spirit that there was no alienation in the unresentful heart he had so deeply wounded: "Go and tell the disciples and Peter" (Mk. 16:7). Even when Judas first revealed himself to his Lord as the betrayer, we believe it was not in bitter irony or rebuke, but in the fullness of pitying tenderness, that Jesus addressed him, "Friend, wherefore art thou come?" (Mt. 26:50). Tears and prayers were his only revenge on the city and scene of his murder. "Beginning at Jerusalem," was the closing illustration of a spirit "not of this world"—a significant parting testimony that in the bosom that uttered it, retaliation had no place.

More than one of the disciples seem to have imbibed much of this *mind* of their Lord. "We owe St. Paul," says Augustine of Hippo (354-430), "to the death of Stephen"—"they stoned Stephen . . . and he kneeled down and cried with a loud voice, 'Lord! lay not this sin to their charge'" (Acts 7:60).

Take another example: The great apostle of the Gentiles felt himself under a painful necessity faithfully to rebuke Peter in the presence of the whole Church. He had recorded that rebuke, too, in one of his epistles. It was thus to be handed down to every age as a permanent and humiliating evidence of the wavering inconstancy of his fellow-laborer. Peter, doubtless, must have felt acutely the severity of the chastisement. Does he resent it? He, too, puts on record, long after, in one of his own epistles a sentence regarding his Rebuker, but it is this—"Our beloved brother Paul" (2 Pet. 3:15)!

Reader, when tempted to utter the harsh word, or give the cutting or hasty answer, seek to check yourself with the question, "Is this the reply my Savior would have given?" If your fellow-men should prove unkind, inconsiderate, ungrateful, be it yours to refer the cause to God. Speak of the faults of others only in prayer; manifesting more sorrow for the sin of the censorious and unkindness, than for the evil inflicted on yourselves. Retaliate! No such word should have a place in the Christian's vocabulary. Retaliate! If I cherish such a spirit toward my brother, how can I meet that brother in heaven? "But ye have not so learned Christ" (Eph. 4:20).

Arm yourselves likewise with the same mind!

O to be like Thee! lowly in spirit,
Holy and harmless, patient and brave;
Meekly enduring cruel reproaches,
Willing to suffer others to save.

O to be like Thee! O to be like Thee,
Blessed Redeemer, pure as Thou art;
Come in Thy sweetness, come in Thy fullness;
Stamp Thine own image deep on my heart.

— Thomas O. Chisholm (1866-1960)

- *Day 21* -
Bearing the Cross

"And he bearing his cross . . ."
John 19:17

When did Jesus bear the cross? Not that moment alone, surely, when the bitter tree was placed on his shoulders, on the way to Golgotha. Its vision may be said to have risen before him in his infant dreams in Bethlehem's cradle. There, rather, its reality began; and he ceased not to carry it, till his work was finished, and the victory won! A cloud, of old, hovered over the mercy seat in the tabernacle and temple. So it was with the Great Antitype—the living Mercy Seat—he had ever a cloud of woe hanging over him. "He carried our sorrows" (Isa. 53:4).

Reader, dwell much and often under the shadow of your Lord's cross, and it will lead you to think lightly of your own! If he gave utterance to not one murmuring word, can you complain? "If we were deeper students of his bitter anguish, we should think less of the ripplings of our waves, amidst his horrible tempest" (David Evans, 1750-1808).

The saint's cross assumes many and diverse shapes. Sometimes it is the bitter trial, the crushing pang of bereavement—desolate households, and aching hearts. Sometimes it is the crucifixion of sin, the determined battle with "lusts which war against the soul" (1 Pet. 2:11). Sometimes it is the resistance of evil maxims and practices of a lying world; vindicating the honor of Christ, in the midst, it may be, of taunt, and abuse, and shame. And as there are different crosses, so there are different ways of bearing them. To some, God says, "put your shoulder to the burden; lift it up, and bear it on; work, and toil, and labor!" To others, he says, "Be still, bear it, and suffer!"

Believer, your cross may be hard to endure; it may involve deep struggles—tears by day, watchings by night. Bear it meekly, patiently, justifying God's wisdom in laying it on you. Rejoice in the assurance that he gives not one atom more of earthly trial than he sees to be really needful; not one redundant thorn pierces your feet. In the very bearing of the cross for his sake, there are mighty compensations. What new views of your Savior's love—his truth, his promises, his sustaining grace, his sufferings, his glory! What new filial nearness, increased delight in prayer, an inner sunshine when it is darkest without! The waves cover you, but underneath them all, are "the everlasting arms" (Dt. 33:27).

Do not look out for a situation without crosses. Be not over anxious about smooth paths—leaving your God, as Orpah did Naomi, just when the cross requires to be carried. Immoderate earthly enjoyments—unbroken earthly prosperity—write upon these, "Beware!" You may live to see them become your greatest trials!

Remember the old saying, "No cross, no crown." The sun of the saint's life generally struggles through weeping clouds. One of the loveliest passages of Scripture is that in which the portals of heaven being opened we overhear this dialogue between two ransomed ones: "And one of the elders answered saying unto me, 'What are these which are arrayed in white robes, and whence came they?' And I said unto him, 'Sir, thou knowest.' And he said to me, 'These are they which came out of great tribulation'" (Rev. 7:13-14).

Arm yourselves likewise with the same mind!

Must Jesus bear the cross alone,
And all the world go free?
No, there's a cross for everyone,
And there's a cross for me.

The consecrated cross I'll bear
Till death shall set me free;
And then go home my crown to wear,
For there's a crown for me.

— Thomas Shepherd (1665-1739)

- *Day 22* -
Holy Zeal

"The zeal of Thine house hath eaten me up."
John 2:17

"Zeal, is a principle; enthusiasm is a feeling. The one is a spark of a sanguine temperament and overheated imagination. The other, a sacred flame kindled at God's altar, and burning in God's shrine," so stated Robert Vaughan (1795-1868). Such was the holy, heavenly zeal of our Great Exemplar; his were no transient out-bursts of ardor, which time cooled and difficulties impeded. His life was one indignant protest against sin—one ceaseless current of un-dying love for souls, which all the malignity of foes, and unkind-ness of friends, could not for one moment divert from its course. Even when he rises from the dead, and we imagine his work at an end, his zeal only mediates fresh deeds of love. "Still his heart and his care," says John Goodwin (1594-1665), "is upon doing more. Having now dispatched that great work on earth, he sends his disci-ples word that he is hastening to heaven as fast as he can, to do an-other" (see John 20:17).

Reader, do you know any thing of this zeal, which many waters could not quench? See that, like your Lord's, it be steady, sober, consistent, undeviating. How many are, like the children of Ephraim, "carrying bows" (Psa. 78:9)—all zealous when zeal demands no sacrifice, but "turning their backs in the day of battle!" Others running well for a time, but gradually hindered, through the benumbing influences of worldliness, selfishness, and sin. Two disciples, apparently equally devoted and zealous, send through Paul, in one of his epistles, a joint Christian salutation: "Luke and Demas greet you" (Col. 4:14). A few years afterward, he writes from his Roman dungeon: "Demas hath forsaken me . . . only Luke is with me." (2 Tim. 4:10-11).

While zeal is commendable, remember the apostle's qualification, "It is good to be zealously affected always in a good thing" (Gal. 4:18). There is in these days much base coin current, called "zeal," which bears not the image and superscription of Jesus. There is zeal for church membership and denomination, zeal for creeds and dogmas, zeal for fantasies and nonessentials. From such *turn aside.* Your Lord stamped with his example and approval no such counterfeits. His zeal was ever brought to bear on two objects, and two objects alone—the glory of God and the good of man. Be it so with you. Enter, first of all (as he did the earthly temple), the sanctuary of your own heart, with "the scourge of small cords" (Jn. 2:15). Drive out every unhallowed intruder there. Do not allow yourself to be deceived. Others may call such jealous soul searching "sanctimoniousness" and "fanaticism." But remember, to be almost saved, is to be altogether lost! To be zealous about everything but "the one thing needful" (Lk. 10:42) is an insult to God and your everlasting interests!

Have a zeal for others. Dying myriads are around you. As a member of the Christian "priesthood" (1 Pet. 2:9), it becomes you to rush in with your censer and incense between the living and the dead, "that the plague may be stayed" (2 Sam. 24:21).

Be it yours to say, "Blessed Jesus! I am yours! Yours only! Yours wholly! Yours forever! I am willing to follow you, and (if need be) to suffer for you. I am ready at your bidding to leave the homestead in the valley, and to face the cutting blasts of the mountain. Take me; use me for your glory. Lord, what will you have me to do?"

Arm yourselves likewise with the same mind!

Awake, my soul, stretch every nerve,
And press with vigor on;
A heavenly race demands thy zeal,
And an immortal crown.

A cloud of witnesses around
Hold thee in full survey;
Forget the steps already trod,
And onward urge thy way.

— Philip Doddridge (1702-1751)

- *Day 23* -
Benevolence

"Who went about doing good."
Acts 10:38

"Christ's great end," says Richard Baxter (1615-1691), "was to save men from their sins; but he delighted to save them from their sorrows."

Jesus' heart bled for human misery. Benevolence brought him from heaven; benevolence followed his steps wherever he went on earth. The journeys of the Divine Philanthropist were marked by tears of thankfulness, and breathings of grateful love. The helpless, the blind, the lame, the desolate, rejoiced at the sound of his footfall. Truly might it be said of him, "When the ear heard me, then it blessed me; and when the eye saw me, it gave witness to me" (Job 29:11).

All suffering hearts were a magnet to Jesus. It was not more his prerogative than his happiness to turn tears into smiles. One of the few pleasures which on earth gladdened the spirit of the "man of sorrows" (Isa. 53:3) was the pleasure of doing good—soothing grief, and alleviating misery. Next to the joy of the widow of Nain when her son was restored, was the joy in the bosom of the Divine Restorer! He often went out of his way to be kind. A journey was not grudged, even if one aching spirit were to be soothed. (Mark 5:1; John, 4:4-5.) Nor were his kindnesses dispensed through the intervention of others. They were all personal acts; his own hand healed, his own voice spoke, his own footsteps lingered on the threshold of bereavement, or at the precincts of the tomb. Ah! had the princes of this world known the loving tenderness and unselfishness of that heart, "they would not have crucified the Lord of glory" (1 Cor. 2:8).

Reader, do you know any thing of such active benevolence? Have you never felt the luxury of doing good? Have you never felt, that in making others happy, you make yourself so; that, by a great law of your being, enunciated by the Divine Patron and Pattern of Benevolence, "it is more blessed to give than to receive" (Acts 20:35)?

Has God enriched you with this world's goods? Seek to view yourself as a consecrated medium for dispensing them to others. Beware alike of stingy hoarding and selfish extravagance. How sad the case of those whose lot God has made thus to abound with temporal mercies, who have gone to the grave unconscious of diminishing one drop of human misery, or making one of the world's myriad aching hearts happier! How the example of Jesus rebukes the cold and calculating kindnesses—the mite-like offerings of many even of his own people whose libation is not like his, from the *brim* of an overflowing cup, but from the *bottom*—from the dregs!

You may have little to give. Your sphere and means may be alike limited. But remember God can be as much glorified by the small saved from the earnings of poverty, as by the splendid benefaction from the lap of plenty. "The Lord loveth a cheerful giver" (2 Cor. 9:7).

The nobler part of Christian benevolence is not vast generosity, lavish monetary sacrifices. "He went about doing good" (Acts 10:38). The merciful visit, the friendly word, the look of sympathy, the cup of cold water, the little unostentatious service, the giving without thought or hope of recompense, the kindly consideration of the poor—anticipating their needs—these are what God values and loves. They are *loans* to himself—tributary streams to the river of his pleasure; they will be acknowledged at last as such—"Ye did it unto Me" (Mt. 25:40).

Arm yourselves likewise with the same mind!

All for Jesus, all for Jesus!
All my being's ransomed powers:
All my thoughts and words and doings,
All my days and all my hours.

Let my hands perform His bidding,
Let my feet run in His ways;
Let my eyes see Jesus only,
Let my lips speak forth His praise.
— Mary D. James (1810-1883)

- *Day 24* -
Firmness in Temptation

"Jesus saith unto him, 'Get thee hence, Satan.'"
Matthew 4:10.

There is an awful intensity of meaning in the words, as applied to Jesus, "he suffered, being tempted" (Heb. 2:18). Though incapable of sin, there was, in the refined sensibilities of his holy nature, that which made temptation unspeakably fearful. What must it have been to confront the Arch-traitor?—to stand face to face with the foe of his throne, and his universe? But the "prince of this world" came, and found "nothing in him" (Jn. 14:30). Billow after billow of Satanic violence spent their fury, in vain, on the Living Rock!

Reader, you have still the same malignant enemy to contend with, assailing you in a thousand insidious forms; marvelously adapting his assaults to your circumstances, your temperament, your mental bias, your master-passion! There is no place where "Satan's seat" is not; "the whole world lieth in the Wicked one" (1 John 5:19). He has his whispers for the ear of childhood; hoary age is not inaccessible to his wiles. "All this will I give thee" (Mt. 4:9) is still his bribe to deny Jesus and to "mind earthly things" (Phil. 3:19). He will meet you in the crowd; he will follow you to the solitude; his is a sleepless vigilance!

Are you bold in repelling him as your Master was? Are you ready with the retort to every foul suggestion, "Get thee hence, Satan" (Mt. 4:10)? Cultivate a tender sensitivity about sin. The finest barometers are the most sensitive. Whatever your besetting frailty is—whatever bitter or baleful passion you are conscious of which aspires to the mastery—watch it, crucify it, *nail it* to your Lord's cross. You may despise the day of *small things*—the Great Adversary does not. He knows the power of *littles*—that little by little consumes and eats out the vigor of the soul. And once the retrograde movement in the spiritual life begins, who can predict where it may end—the going on "from weakness to weakness," instead of "from strength to strength."

Make no compromises; never join in the ungodly amusement, or venture on the questionable path, with the plea, "It does me no harm." The Israelites, on entering Canaan, instead of obeying the Divine injunction of extirpating their enemies, made a hollow truce with them. What was the result? Years upon years of tedious warfare. "They were scourges in their sides, and thorns in their eyes (Jos. 23:13). It is quaintly but truthfully said by an old writer, "The candle will never burn clear, while there is a thief in it. Sin indulged, in the conscience, is like Jonah in the ship, which causeth such a tempest, that the conscience is like a troubled sea, whose waters cannot rest" (Thomas Brooks, 1608-1680).

"Keep," then, "thy heart with all diligence," or, as it is in the forcible original Hebrew, "keep thy heart above all keeping, for out of it are the issues of life." (Prov. 4:23).

Let this ever be your preservative against temptation, "How would Jesus have acted here? Would he not have recoiled, like the sensitive plant, from the remotest contact with sin? Can I think of dishonoring him by tampering with his enemy; incurring from his own lips the bitter reflection of injured love, 'I am wounded in the house of my friends'" (Zech. 13:6)?

Jesus tells us the secret of our preservation and safety, "Simon! Simon! Satan hath desired to have thee, that he might sift thee as wheat; but I have prayed for thee that thy faith fail not" (Lk. 22:32).

Arm yourselves likewise with the same mind!

Beware of Peter's word,
Nor confidently say,
"I never will deny the Lord,"
But "grant I never may."

Man's wisdom is to seek
His strength in God alone;
And e'en an angel would be weak,
Who trusted in his own.

— William Cowper (1731-1800)

- *Day 25* -
Receiving Sinners

"This man receiveth sinners."
Luke 15:2

The ironical taunt of proud and censorious Pharisees formed the glory of him who came, "not to call the righteous, but sinners, to repentance" (Mt. 9:13). Publicans and outcasts, those covered with a deeper than any bodily leprosy—laid bare their wounds to the Great Physician, and as conscious guilt and timid penitence crept abashed and imploring to his feet, they found nothing but a forgiving and a gracious welcome!

His ways were not as man's ways! The "watchmen," in the Canticles, "smote" the disconsolate one seeking her lost Lord; they tore off her veil, mocking with chilling unkindness her anguished tears (Sg. 5:7). Not so "the Chief Shepherd and Bishop of souls" (1 Pet. 5:4). "This man receiveth sinners"! See Nicodemus, stealing under the shadows of night to elude observation—type of the thousand thousand who in every age have gone trembling in their night of sin and sorrow to this heavenly Friend! Does Jesus punish his timidity by shutting his door against him, spurning him from his presence?

"He will not break the bruised reed; he will not quench the smoking flax" (Isa. 42:3).

And he is still the same! He who arrested a persecutor in his blasphemies, and tuned the lips of an expiring felon with faith and love, is at this hour standing, with all the garnered treasures of Redemption in his hand, proclaiming, "him that cometh unto Me, I will in no wise cast out" (Jn. 6:37).

Are we from this to think lightly of sin or, by example and conduct, to explain away and overlook its enormity? Not so. Sin, as sin, can never be sufficiently stamped with the brand of approval. But we must seek carefully to distinguish between the offence and the offender. Nothing should be done on our part, by word or deed, to mock the penitential sighings of a guilty spirit, or send the trembling outcast away, with the despairing feeling of *no hope*. "This man receiveth sinners," and shall not we? Does he suffer the sundry dregs of human depravity to crouch unbidden at his feet, and to gaze on his forgiving countenance with the uplifted eye of hope, and shall we dare to deal out harsh, and severe, and crushing verdicts on an offending (it may be a deeply offending) brother? Shall we pronounce "crimson" and "scarlet" sins and sinners beyond the pale of mercy, when Jesus does not?

Nay, rather, when wretchedness, and depravity, and backsliding cross our path, let it not be with the bitter taunt or the ironical retort that we bid them away. Let us bear, endure, remonstrate, deal tenderly. Jesus did so, Jesus does so! Ah! If we had within us his unconquerable love of souls, his yearning desire for the everlasting happiness of sinners, we should be more frequently in earnest protest and affectionate appeal with those who have hitherto got no other than harsh thoughts and repulsive words. If this "mind" really were in us, "which was also in him," we should more frequently ask ourselves, "Have I done all I might have done to pluck this brand from the burning! Have I remembered what grace has wrought, what grace can do?"

"Brethren, if any of you do err from the truth, and one convert him, let him know, that he which converteth the sinner from the error of his way shall save a soul from death, and shall hide a multitude of sins" (Ja. 5:19).

Arm yourselves likewise with the same mind!

Rescue the perishing, care for the dying,
Snatch them in pity from sin and the grave;
Weep o'er the erring one, lift up the fallen,
Tell them of Jesus, the mighty to save.

Down in the human heart, crushed by the tempter,
Feelings lie buried that grace can restore;
Touched by a loving heart, wakened by kindness,
Chords that were broken will vibrate once more.

— Fanny Crosby (1820-1915)

- *Day 26* -
Guilelessness

"Neither was guile found in his mouth."
1 Peter 2:22

How rare, and all the more beautiful because of its rarity, is a purely guileless spirit! A crystalline medium through which the transparent light of heaven comes and goes—open, candid, just, honorable, sincere—scorning every unfair dealing, every hollow pretension, every narrow prejudice. Wherever such characters exist, they are like "apples of gold in pictures of silver" (Prov. 25:11).

Such, in all the loveliness of sinless perfection, was the Son of God! His guilelessness shining the more conspicuously amid the artful and malignant subtlety alike of men and demons. Passing by manifold instances in the course of his ministry, look at its manifestation as the hour of his death approached. When, on the night of his apprehension, he confronts the assassin band, in meek majesty he puts the question, "Whom seek ye?" They say to him, "Jesus of Nazareth." In guileless innocence, he replies, "I am he!" (Jn. 18:4-5). "Art thou the King of the Jews?" asks Pilate, a few hours after. An evasive answer might again have purchased immunity from suffering and indignity, but once more the lips which scorned the semblance of evasion reply, "Thou sayest" (Mk. 15:2).

How he loved the same spirit in his people! "Behold," said he, of Nathanael, "an Israelite indeed, in whom is no guile!" (Jn. 1:47). That upright man had, we may suppose, been day after day kneeling in prayer under his fig tree, with an open and candid spirit: Musing on the law he taught, and waiting for the Lord he loved.

See how the Savior honored him—setting his own Divine seal on the loveliness of this same spirit! Take one other example: when the startling, saddening announcement is made to the disciples, "One of you shall betray me" (Jn. 13:21), they do not accuse one another; they attempt to throw no suspicion on Judas; each in trembling apprehension suspects only his own treacherous heart, "Lord, is it I?"

How much of a different "mind" is there abroad! In the school of the world (this *painted world*), how much is there of what is called policy, double-dealing—accomplishing its ends by tortuous means; outward, artificial polish, often only a cloak for baseness and selfishness—in the daily interchange of business, one seeking to overreach the other by wily arts, sacrificing principle for temporal advantage. There is nothing so derogatory to religion as anything allied to such a spirit among Christ's people—any such blot on the *living epistles*. "Ye are the light of the world" (Mt. 5:14). That world is a quick observer. It is sharp to detect inconsistencies—slow to forget them. The true Christian has been likened to an anagram—you ought to be able to read him up and down, every way!

Be all reality, no counterfeit. Do not pass for current coin what is base alloy. Let transparent honor and sincerity regulate all your dealings; despise all meanness, avoid the sinister motive, the underhand dealing; aim at that unswerving love of truth that would scorn to stoop to base conformity and unworthy equivocations; live more under the power of the purifying and ennobling influences of the gospel. Take its golden rule as the matchless directory for the daily transactions of life: "Whatsoever ye would that men should do to you, do ye even so to them" (Mt. 7:12).

Arm yourselves likewise with the same mind!

May the mind of Christ, my Savior,
Live in me from day to day,
By His love and power controlling
All I do and say.

May the Word of God dwell richly
In my heart from hour to hour,
So that all may see I triumph
Only through His power.

— Kate B. Wilkinson (1859-1928)

- *Day 27* -
Activity in Duty

"I must work the works of him that sent me, while it is day;
the night cometh, when no man can work."
John 9:4

How constant and unremitting was Jesus in the service of his heavenly Father! "He rose a great while before day" (Mk. 1:35), and, when his secret communion was over, his public work began. It mattered not to him where he was: whether on the bosom of the deep, or a mountain slope, in the desert, or at a well-side, the "gracious words" ever "proceeded out of his mouth" (Lk. 4:22). We find, on one touching occasion, exhausted nature sinking, after a day of unremitting duty, in crossing in a vessel, the Lake of Tiberias—"he fell asleep" (Mt. 8:24). He redeemed every precious moment. His words to the Pharisee seem a formula for all, "Simon, I have somewhat to say unto thee" (Lk. 7:40).

Oh, how our most unceasing activities pale into nothing before such an example as this! Would that we could remember that each of us has some great mission to perform for God, that religion is not a thing of dreamy sentimentalism, but of energetic practical action;

moreover, that no trade, no profession, no position, however high or however humble in the scale of society, can disqualify for this life of Christian activity and usefulness! Who were the writers in the Bible? We have among them a king, a lawgiver, a herdsman, a publican, a physician! Nor is it to high spheres, or to great services only, that God looks. The widow's mite and Mary's alabaster box of ointment are recorded as examples for imitation by the Holy Spirit, while many more generous deeds are passed by unrecorded. We believe that God says, regarding the attempt of many a humble Christian to serve him by active duty, "I saw that effort, that feeble effort to serve and glorify Me; it was the very feebleness of it I loved!"

Did it never strike you, notwithstanding the dignity of Christ, and the activity of Christ, how little success comparatively he met with in his public work? We read of no numerous conversions, no Pentecostal revivals in the course of his ministry. May not this well encourage us in the absence of great outward results? He sets up no higher standard than this—"She hath done what she could" (Mk. 14:8). An artist may be great in painting a peasant as well as a king—it is the way he does it. Yes, and if laid aside from the activities of the Christian life, we can equally glorify God by passive endurance. "Who am I," said Martin Luther (1483-1546), when he witnessed the patience of a great sufferer; "who am I? A wordy preacher in comparison with this great doer."

Reader, forget not the motive of our motto verse, "The night cometh!" Soon our tale shall be told; our little day is flitting fast, the shadows of night are falling. "Our span length of time," as Samuel Rutherford (1600-1661) says, "will come to an inch." What if the eleventh hour should strike after having been "all the day idle"?

A long lifetime of opportunities allowed to pass unemployed and unimproved, and absolutely nothing done for God! A judgment day come—our golden moments squandered, our talents untraded on, our work undone—met at the bar of heaven with the withering repulse, "Inasmuch as ye did it not" (Mt. 25:45). "The time we have lost," says Richard Baxter (1615-1691), "can not be recalled; should we not then redeem and improve the little that remains? If a traveler sleep or trifle most of the day, he must travel so much the faster in the evening, or fall short of his journey's end."

Arm yourselves likewise with the same mind!

Workman of God! O lose not heart,
But learn what God is like;
And in the darkest battlefield
Thou shalt know where to strike.

Thrice blest is he to whom is giv'n
The instinct that can tell
That God is on the field, when He
Is most invisible.

— Frederick W. Faber (1814-1863)

- *Day 28* -
Committing our Way to God

"But committed himself to him that judgeth righteously."
1 Peter 2:23

With what perfect and entire confidence did Jesus commit himself to his heavenly Father's guidance! He loved to call him, "My Father!" There was music in that name, which enabled him to face the most trying hour, and to drink the most bitter cup. The scoffing taunt arose at the scene of crucifixion: "He trusted in God; let him deliver him now . . ." (Mt. 27:43). It failed to shake, for one moment, his unswerving confidence, even when the sensible tokens of the Divine presence were withdrawn; the realized consciousness of God's abiding love sustained him still: "My God! my God" (Mt. 27:46).

How many a perplexity should we save ourselves by thus implicitly "committing ourselves," as he did, to God! In seasons of darkness and trouble—when our way is shut up with thorns, to lift the confiding eye of faith to him, and say, "I am oppressed, undertake for me!" How blessed to feel that he directs all that befalls us; that no contingencies can frustrate his plans; that the way he leads us is not

The Mind of Christ

only a *right way*, but, with all its briers and thorns—its tears and trials—it is the right way!

The result of such a habitual placing ourselves on the Lord will be a deep, abiding peace; any ripple will only be on the surface—no more. It is the bosom of the ocean alone which the storm ruffles; all beneath is a serene, settled calm. So "Thou wilt keep him, oh God, in perfect peace, whose mind is stayed on Thee" (Isa. 26:3).

"The Lord is my shepherd, I shall not want" (Psa. 23:1). I shall be content alike with what he appoints or withholds. I cannot wrong that love with one shadow of suspicion! I have his own pledged promise of unchanging faithfulness, that "all things work together for good to them that love him" (Rom. 8:28). Often there are earthly sorrows hard to bear—the unkind accusation, when it was least merited or expected; the estrangement of tried and trusted friends, the failure of cherished hopes, favorite plans broken up, plans of usefulness demolished, the gourd breeding its own worm and withering (see Jon. 4:7). Commit thy *cause* and thy *way* to God! We little know what tenderness there is in the blast of the rough wind; what *needs be* are folded under the wings of the storm! "All is well," because all is from him. "Events are God's," says Samuel Rutherford (1600-1661), "let him sit at his own helm, that moderateth all."

Christian, look back on your checkered path. How wondrously has he threaded you through the mazy way—disappointing your fears, realizing your hopes! Are evils looming through the mists of the future? Do not anticipate the trials of tomorrow, to aggravate those of today. Leave the morrow with him, who has promised, by "casting all your care on him, to care for you" (1 Pet. 5:7). No affliction will be sent greater than you can bear. His voice will be heard stealing from the bosom of the threatening cloud, "Be still, and know that I am God" (Psa. 46:10).

"My Father!" With such a word, you can stretch out your neck for any yoke. As with Israel of old, he will make those very waves that may now be so threatening, a fenced wall on every side! "Rest in the Lord, and wait patiently for him" (Psa. 37:7). "In all thy ways acknowledge him, and he shall direct thy paths" (Prov. 3:6).

Arm yourselves likewise with the same mind!

Day by day, and with each passing moment,
Strength I find to meet my trials here;
Trusting in my Father's wise bestowment,
I've no cause for worry or for fear.
He, whose heart is kind beyond all measure,
Gives unto each day what He deems best,
Lovingly its part of pain and pleasure,
Mingling toil with peace and rest.

Every day the Lord Himself is near me,
With a special mercy for each hour;
All my cares He fain would bear and cheer me,
He whose name is Counselor and Pow'r.
The protection of His child and treasure
Is a charge that on Himself He laid;
"As thy days, thy strength shall be in measure,"
This the pledge to me He made.

— Lina Sandell Berg (1832-1903)

- *Day 29* -
Love of Unity

"That they all may be one."
John 17:21

Surely there is nothing for which Christian churches have such cause to hang their harps on the willows, as the extent to which the Shibboleth (see Jug. 12:6) of sectarianism is heard in the camp of the faithful—sectarianism rearing its *untempered* walls within the Temple gates!

How different the mind of Jesus! Sent "to the lost sheep of the house of Israel" (Mt. 15:24), he was never found disowning other sheep not of that *fold*. "Them also will I bring" (Jn. 10:16), was an assertion continually illustrated by his deeds. Take one example: The woman of Samaria revealed what, alas! is too common in the world—a total absence of all real religion, along with an ardent zeal for her sect. She was living in open sin, yet she was all alive to the nice distinction between a Jew and a Samaritan—between Mount Gerizim and Mount Zion: "How is it that thou, being a Jew, askest drink of me, who am a woman of Samaria"? (Jn. 4:9). Did Jesus sanction or reciprocate her sectarianism? Did he leave her bigotry unrebuked? Hear his reply: "If thou knewest the gift of God, and who it is that saith to thee, Give me to drink; thou wouldst have asked of him, and he would have given thee" (Jn. 4:10). He would have allowed no such narrow-minded exclusiveness to have interfered with the interchange of kindly civilities with a stranger. No, he would have given you, better than all, the "living water" which "springeth up to everlasting life" (Jn. 4:14).

How sad, that when the enemy is "coming in like a flood" (Isa. 59:19)—the ranks of apostasy and infidelity linked in fatal and formidable confederacy—that the soldiers of Christ are forced to meet the assault with standards soiled and mutilated by internal feuds! "Uniformity" there may not be, but "unity," in the true sense of the word, there ought to be. We may be clad in different *garments*, but let us stand side by side, and rank by rank, fighting the battles of our Lord. We may be different branches of the seven golden candlesticks, varying and diversified in outward form and workmanship, but let us combine in "showing forth the praises of him" (1 Pet. 2:9) who recognizes, as the one true "churchmanship," fidelity in shining for his glory "as lights in the world" (Phil. 2:15). How can we read the 13th chapter of 1 Corinthians, and then think of our divisions? "How miserable," says Edward Bickersteth (1825-1906), "would an hospital be, if each patient were to be so offended with his neighbor's disease, as to differ with him on account of it, instead of trying to alleviate it!"

Ah, if we had more real communion with our Savior, should we not have more real communion with one another? If Christians would dip their arrows more in "the balm of Gilead," would there not be fewer wounds in the body of Christ? "How that word *toleration* is used amongst us," said one who drank deeper than most, of his Master's spirit. "How we tolerate one another; Dissenters tolerate Churchmen, and Churchmen tolerate Dissenters! Oh! hateful word! TOLERATE one for whom Jesus died! Tolerate one whom he bears upon his heart! Tolerate a temple of the living God! Oh! there ought to be that in the word which should make us feel ashamed before God!"

Arm yourselves likewise with the same mind!

Blest be the tie that binds
Our hearts in Christian love;
The fellowship of kindred minds
Is like to that above.

Before our Father's throne
We pour our ardent prayers;
Our fears, our hopes, our aims are one
Our comforts and our cares.

We share each other's woes,
Our mutual burdens bear;
And often for each other flows
The sympathizing tear.

— John Fawcett (1740-1817)

- *Day 30* -
Not of the World

"I am not of the world."
John 17:14

In one sense it was not so. Jesus did not seek to maintain his holiness intact and unspotted by avoiding contact with the world. He mingled familiarly in its busy crowds. He frowned on none of its innocent enjoyments; he fostered, by his example, no love of seclusion; he gave no warrant or encouragement to mortified pride, or disappointed hopes, to rush from its duties; yet, with all this, what a halo of heavenliness encircled his pathway through it!

"I am from above," was breathed in his every look, and word, and action, from the time when he lay in the slumbers of guileless infancy in his Bethlehem cradle, until he said, "I leave the world, and go to my Father" (Jn. 16:10). He had moved uncontaminated through its varied scenes, like the sunbeam, which, whatever it touches, remains as unsullied, as when it issues from its great fountain.

But though himself in his sinless nature *unconquerable* by temptation—immutably secure from the world's malignant influences—it is all worthy of note, as an example to us, that he never unnecessarily braved these. He knew the seducing spell that same world would exercise on his people, of whom, with touching sympathy, he says, "These are in the world" (Jn. 17:11). He knew the many who would be involved and ensnared in its subtle worship, who, minding *earthly things*, would seek to slake their thirst at polluted streams!

Reader, the great problem you have to solve, Jesus has solved for you—to be "in the world, and yet not of it." To abandon it, would be a dereliction of duty. It would be servants deserting their work, soldiers flying from the battlefield. Live in it, that while you live the world may feel the better for you. Die, that when you die, the world, the Church, may feel your loss and cherish your example! On its cares and duties, its trusts and responsibilities, its employments and enjoyments, inscribe the motto, "The world passeth away" (I Jn. 2:17)!

Beware of every thing in the world that would tend to deaden spirituality of heart, unfitting the mind for serious thought, lowering the standard of Christian duty, and inducing a perilous conformity to its false manners, habits, tastes, and principles. As the best antidote to the love of the world, let the inner vacuum of the heart be filled with the love of God. Seek to feel the nobility of your regenerated nature, that you have a nobler heritage to care for than the transitory glories which encircle an indivisible point, a fugitive atom.

How can I mix with the potsherds of the earth? Once, "I lay among the pots;" now, I am "like a dove, whose wings are covered with silver, and her feathers with yellow gold" (Psa. 68:13). Stranger, pilgrim, sojourner—"my citizenship is in heaven" (Phil. 3:20). Why covet tinsel honors and glories? Why be solicitous about the smiles of that which knew not (nay, which frowned on) its Lord? "Paul calls it," says an old writer, "*schema* (a mathematical figure), which is a mere notion, and nothing in substance" (Thomas Brooks, 1608-1680).

Live above the world's corroding cares and anxieties, remembering the description Jesus gives of his own true people, "They are not of the world, even as I am not of the world" (Jn. 17:16).

Arm yourselves likewise with the same mind!

Take the world, but give me Jesus,
All its joys are but a name;
But His love abideth ever,
Through eternal years the same.

Take the world, but give me Jesus.
In His cross my trust shall be,
Till, with clearer, brighter vision,
Face to face my Lord I see.

— Fanny Crosby (1820-1915)

- *Day 31* -
Calmness in Death

"Father, into Thy hands I commend my spirit."
Luke 23:46

In the death of Jesus there were elements of fearfulness, which the believer can know nothing of. It was with him the execution of a *penal* sentence. The sins of an elect world were bearing him down! The very voice of his God was giving the tremendous summons, "Awake, O sword, against my shepherd" (Zech. 13:7). Yet his was a death of peace, nay, of triumph! Ere he closed his eyes, light broke through the curtains of thick darkness. In the calm composure of filial confidence he breathed away his soul, "Father, into Thy hands I commend My spirit!" What was the secret of such tranquility? This is his own key to it: "I have glorified Thee on the earth; I have finished the work which Thou gavest me to do" (Jn. 17:4).

Reader, will it be so with you at your dying hour? Will your "work" be done? Have you already fled to Jesus? Are you reposing in him as your only Savior, and following him as your only pattern? Then, let death overtake you when it may, you will have nothing to do but to die! The grave will be radiant with his presence and smile. He will be standing there as he did by his own tomb of old, pointing to yours, inhabited with angel forms, nay, himself as the Precursor, showing you the path of life! There can be no true peace till the fear of death be conquered by the sense of sins forgiven, through the *blood of the Cross.* "Not till then," as one has it, "will you be able to be a quiet spectator of the open grave at the bottom of the hill which you are soon to descend." "The sting of death is sin, but thanks be to God who giveth us the victory through the Lord Jesus Christ (1 Cor. 56-57).

Seek now to live in the enjoyment of greater filial nearness to your covenant God; and thus, when the hour of departure does come, you will be able, without irreverence, to take the very words of your dying Lord, and make them your own: "FATHER, into Thy hands I commend my spirit." FATHER, I'm coming HOME! The heart of the child leaping at the thought of the paternal home, and the paternal welcome! "Son, thou art ever with me, and all that I have is thine" (Lk. 15:31).

It is said of Archbishop Leighton (1643-1715), that he "was always happiest when, from the shaking of the prison doors, he was led to hope that some of those brisk blasts would throw them open, and give him the release he coveted." Christian, can you dread that which your Savior has already vanquished? Death! It is as the angel to Peter, breaking the dungeon doors, and leading to a new day. It is going to the world of your birthright, and leaving the one of your exile; it is the soldier at night-fall, lying down in his tent in peace, waiting the morning to receive his laurels.

Oh, to be ever living in a state of holy preparation, the mental eye gazing on the vista-view of an opening heaven, feeling that every moment is bringing us nearer and nearer that happy Home! Soon to be within reach of the heavenly threshold, in sight of the Throne! Soon to be bending in adoring rapture with the Church triumphant, bathing in floods of infinite glory! "LIKE HIM"—"seeing HIM as he is" (1 Jn. 3:2). And that for Ever and Ever!

"And every man that hath this hope in him
purifieth himself, even as he is pure."
1 John 3:3

"Leaving us an example that ye should follow his steps."
1 Peter 2:21

Finish, then, Thy new creation;
Pure and spotless let us be.
Let us see Thy great salvation
Perfectly restored in Thee,
Changed from glory into glory,
Till in heaven we take our place,
Till we cast our crowns before Thee,
Lost in wonder, love, and praise.

— Charles Wesley (1707-1788)

www.ingramcontent.com/pod-product-compliance
Lightning Source LLC
Chambersburg PA
CBHW021205020426
42331CB00003B/207